180 Days of Social-Emotional Learning

for Fourth Grade

Kristin Kemp, M.A.Ed.

Consultants

Kris Hinrichsen, M.A.T., NBCT
Teacher and Educational Consultant
Anchorage School District

Amy Zoque
Teacher and Instructional Coach
Ontario Montclair School District

Publishing Credits

Corinne Burton, M.A.Ed., *Publisher*
Emily R. Smith, M.A.Ed., *VP of Content Development*
Lynette Ordoñez, *Content Specialist*
David Slayton, *Assistant Editor*
Jill Malcolm, *Multimedia Specialist*

Image Credits: all images from iStock and/or Shutterstock

Social-Emotional Learning Framework

The CASEL SEL framework and competencies were used in the development of this series.
© 2020 The Collaborative for Academic, Social, and Emotional Learning

A division of Teacher Created Materials
5482 Argosy Avenue
Huntington Beach, CA 92649-1039
www.tcmpub.com/shell-education
ISBN 978-1-0876-4973-3
© 2022 Shell Educational Publishing, Inc
Printed in China 51497

Table of Contents

Introduction

"SEL is the process through which all young people and adults acquire and apply the knowledge, skills, and attitudes to develop healthy identities, manage emotions and achieve personal and collective goals, feel and show empathy for others, establish and maintain supportive relationships, and make responsible and caring decisions." (CASEL 2020)

Social-emotional learning (SEL) covers a wide range of skills that help people improve themselves and get fulfilment from their relationships. They are the skills that help propel us into the people we want to be. SEL skills give people the tools to think about the future and manage the day-to-day goal setting to get where we want to be.

The National Commission for Social, Emotional, and Academic Development (2018) noted that children need many skills, attitudes, and values to succeed in school, future careers, and life. "They require skills such as paying attention, setting goals, collaboration and planning for the future. They require attitudes such as internal motivation, perseverance, and a sense of purpose. They require values such as responsibility, honesty, and integrity. They require the abilities to think critically, consider different views, and problem solve." Explicit SEL instruction will help students develop and hone these important skills, attitudes, and values.

Daniel Goleman (2005), a social scientist who popularized SEL, adds, "Most of us have assumed that the kind of academic learning that goes on in school has little or nothing to do with one's emotions or social environment. Now, neuroscience is telling us exactly the opposite. The emotional centers of the brain are intricately interwoven with the neocortical areas involved in cognitive learning." As adults, we may find it difficult to focus on work after a bad day or a traumatic event. Similarly, student learning is impacted by their emotions. By teaching students how to deal with their emotions in a healthy way, they will reap the benefits academically as well.

SEL is doing the work to make sure students can be successful at home, with their friends, at school, in sports, in relationships, and in life. The skills are typically separated into five competencies: self-awareness, self-management, social awareness, relationship skills, and responsible decision-making.

Introduction *(cont.)*

Social-Emotional Competencies

SELF-MANAGEMENT
Manage your emotions, thoughts, and behaviors. Set and work toward goals.

SOCIAL AWARENESS
Take on the perspectives of others, especially those who are different from you. Understand societal expectations and know where to get support.

SELF-AWARENESS
Recognize your own emotions, thoughts, and values. Assess your strengths and weaknesses. Have a growth mindset.

SEL COMPETENCIES

RESPONSIBLE DECISION-MAKING
Make positive choices based on established norms. Understand and consider consequences.

RELATIONSHIP SKILLS
Establish and maintain relationships with others. Communicate effectively and negotiate conflict as necessary.

Each SEL competency helps support child development in life-long learning. SEL helps students develop the skills to have rich connections with their emotional lives and build robust emotional vocabularies. These competencies lead to some impressive data to support students being successful in school and in life.

- Students who learn SEL skills score an average of 11 percentage points higher on standardized tests.

- They are less likely to get office referrals and will spend more time in class.

- These students are more likely to want to come to school and report being happier while at school.

- Educators who teach SEL skills report a 77 percent increase in job satisfaction. (Durlack, et al. 2011)

Your SEL Skills

Educators, parents, and caretakers have a huge part to play as students develop SEL skills. Parker Palmer (2007) reminds us that what children do is often a reflection of what they see and experience. When you stay calm, name your feelings, practice clear communication, and problem-solve in a way that students see, then they reflect that modeling in their own relationships. As you guide students in how to handle conflicts, you can keep a growth mindset and know that with practice, your students can master any skill.

Introduction *(cont.)*

Scenarios

There are many benefits to teaching SEL, from how students behave at home to how they will succeed in life. Let's think about how children with strong SEL skills would react to common life experiences.

At Home

Kyle wakes up. He uses self-talk and says to himself, *I am going to do my best today.* He gets out of bed, picks out his own clothes to wear, and gets ready. As he sits down for breakfast, his little sister knocks over his glass of milk. He thinks, *Uggh, she is so messy! But that's ok—it was just an accident.* Then, he tells his parent and helps clean up the mess.

When his parent picks Kyle up from school, Kyle asks how they are feeling and answers questions about how his day has gone. He says that he found the reading lesson hard, but he used deep breathing and asked questions to figure out new words today.

As his family is getting dinner ready, he sees that his parent is making something he really doesn't like. He stomps his foot in protest, and then he goes to sit in his room for a while. When he comes out, he asks if they can make something tomorrow that he likes.

When he is getting ready for bed, he is silly and playful. He wants to read and point out how each person in the book is feeling. His parent asks him how he would handle the problem the character is facing, and then they talk about the situation.

At School

Cynthia gets to school a little late, and she has to check into the office. Cynthia is embarrassed about being late but feels safe at school and knows that the people there will welcome her with kindness. She steps into her room, and her class pauses to welcome her. Her teacher says, "I'm so glad you are here today."

Cynthia settles into her morning work. After a few minutes, she comes to a problem she doesn't know how to solve. After she gives it her best try, she asks her teacher for some help. Her teacher supports her learning, and Cynthia feels proud of herself for trying.

As lunchtime nears, Cynthia realizes she forgot her lunch in the car. She asks her teacher to call her mom. Her mom says she can't get away and that Cynthia is going to have to eat the school lunch today. Cynthia is frustrated but decides that she is not going to let it ruin her day.

As she is getting ready for school to end, her teacher invites the class to reflect about their day. What is something they are proud of? What is something they wished they could do again? Cynthia thinks about her answers and shares with the class.

These are both pretty dreamy children. The reality is that the development of SEL skills happens in different ways. Some days, students will shock you by how they handle a problem. Other times, they will dig in and not use the skills you teach them. One of the benefits of teaching SEL is that when a student is melting down, your mindset shifts to *I wonder how I can help them learn how to deal with this* rather than *I'm going to punish them so they don't do this again.* Viewing discipline as an opportunity to teach rather than punish is critical for students to learn SEL.

How to Use This Book

Using the Practice Pages

This series is designed to support the instruction of SEL. It is not a curriculum. The activities will help students practice, learn, and grow their SEL skills. Each week is set up for students to practice all five SEL competencies.

 Day 1—Self-Awareness

 Day 2—Self-Management

 Day 3—Social Awareness

 Day 4—Relationship Skills

 Day 5—Responsible Decision-Making

Each of the five competencies has subcategories that are used to target specific skills each day. See the chart on pages 10–11 for a list of which skills are used throughout the book.

Each week also has a theme. These themes rotate and are repeated several times throughout the book. The following themes are included in this book:

- self
- family
- friends
- school
- neighborhood
- community
- state
- country

This book also features one week that focuses on online safety.

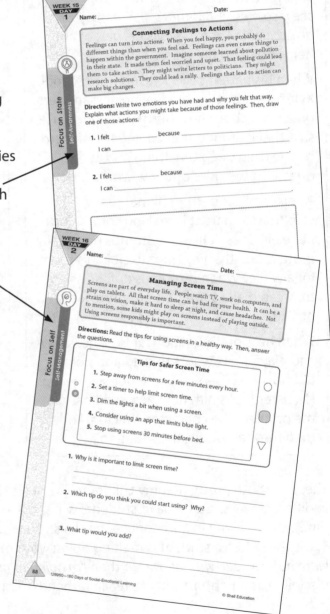

How to Use This Book *(cont.)*

Using the Resources

Rubrics for connecting to self, relating to others, and making decisions can be found on pages 199–201 and in the Digital Resources. Use the rubrics to consider student work. Be sure to share these rubrics with students so that they know what is expected of them.

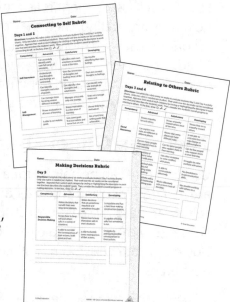

Diagnostic Assessment

Educators can use the pages in this book as diagnostic assessments. The data analysis tools included with this book enable teachers or parents/caregivers to quickly assess students' work and monitor their progress. Educators can quickly see which skills students may need to target further to develop proficiency.

Students will learn how to connect with their own emotions, how to connect with the emotions of others, and how to make good decisions. Assess student learning in each area using the rubrics on pages 199–201. Then, record their overall progress on the analysis sheets on pages 202–204. These charts are also provided in the Digital Resources as PDFs and Microsoft Excel® files.

To Complete the Analyses:

- Write or type students' names in the far-left column. Depending on the number of students, more than one copy of each form may be needed.

- The weeks in which students should be assessed are indicated in the first rows of the charts. Students should be assessed at the ends of those weeks.

- Review students' work for the day(s) indicated in the corresponding rubric. For example, if using the Making Decisions Analysis sheet for the first time, review students' work from Day 5 for all six weeks.

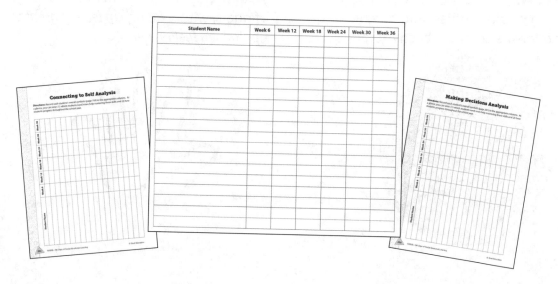

Integrating SEL into Your Teaching

Student self-assessment is key for SEL skills. If students can make accurate evaluations of how they are feeling, then they can work to manage their emotions. If they can manage their emotions, they are more likely to have better relationship skills and make responsible decisions. Children can self-assess from a very young age. The earlier you get them into this practice, the more they will use it and benefit from it for the rest of their lives. The following are some ways you can quickly and easily integrate student self-assessment into your daily routines.

Feelings Check-Ins

Using a scale can be helpful for a quick check-in. After an activity, ask students to rate how they are feeling. Focusing students' attention on how they are feeling helps support their self-awareness. Discuss how students' feelings change as they do different things. Provide students with a visual scale to support these check-ins. These could be taped to their desks or posted in your classroom. Full-color versions of the following scales can be found in the Digital Resources.

- **Emoji:** Having students point to different emoji faces is an easy way to use a rating scale with young students.

- **Symbols:** Symbols, such as weather icons, can also represent students' emotions.

- **Color Wheel:** A color wheel, where different colors represent different emotions, is another effective scale.

- **Numbers:** Have students show 1–5 fingers, with 5 being *I'm feeling great* to 1 being *I'm feeling awful*.

Integrating SEL into Your Teaching *(cont.)*

Reflection

Reflecting is the process of looking closely or deeply at something. When you prompt students with reflection questions, you are supporting this work. Here is a list of questions to get the reflection process started:

- What did you learn from this work?

- What are you proud of in this piece?

- What would you have done differently?

- What was the most challenging part?

- How could you improve this work?

- How did other people help you finish this work?

- How will doing your best on this assignment help you in the future?

Pan Balance

Have students hold out their arms on both sides of their bodies. Ask them a reflection question that has two possible answers. Students should respond by tipping one arm lower than the other (as if one side of the scale is heavier). Here are some example questions:

- Did you talk too much or too little?

- Were you distracted or engaged?

- Did you rush or take too much time?

- Did you stay calm or get angry?

- Was your response safe or unsafe?

Calibrating Student Assessments

Supporting student self-assessment means calibrating their thinking. You will have students who make mistakes but evaluate themselves as though they have never made a mistake in their lives. At the other end of the spectrum, you will likely see students who will be too hard on themselves. In both these cases, having a periodic calibration can help to support accuracy in their evaluations. The *Calibrating Student Assessments* chart is provided in the Digital Resources (calibrating.pdf).

Teaching Assessment

In addition to assessing students, consider the effectiveness of your own instruction. The *Teaching Rubric* can be found in the Digital Resources (teachingrubric.pdf). Use this tool to evaluate your SEL instruction. You may wish to complete this rubric at different points throughout the year to track your progress.

Skills Alignment

Each activity in this book is aligned to a CASEL competency. Within each competency, students will learn a variety of skills. Here are some of the important skills students will practice during the year.

Self-Awareness

Identifying Emotions	Developing Interests
Understanding Culture	Core Values
Growth Mindset	Understanding Emotional Intensity
Integrity	Being Open-Minded
Self-Advocacy	Examining Biases and Prejudices
Personal and Social Identities	Honesty

Self-Management

Managing Emotions	Self-Discipline
Using Self-Talk	Trying New Things
Helping Others	Planning and Organization
Stress Management	I-Messages
Setting Goals	Schedules
Overcoming Fear	

Social Awareness

Body Language	Showing Concern for Others
Gratitude	Helping Others
Understanding Different Rules	Social Norms
Noticing Needs	Understanding Others' Emotions
Fairness	Predicting Others' Feelings
Taking Others' Perspectives	Influencing Others
Recognizing Others' Strengths	

Skills Alignment *(cont.)*

Relationship Skills

Nonverbal Communication	Developing Positive Relationships
Teamwork	Standing Up for Others
Resolving Conflicts	Resisting Peer Pressure
Leadership	Decoding Messages
Appreciating Other Cultures	Communication Helpers and Blockers
Seeking Help	Communication Feedback
Effective Communication	Paraphrasing
Leadership	Active Listening

Responsible Decision-Making

Recognizing Problems	Reflecting
Trying New Things	Evaluating Impact
Making Good Decisions	Solving Problems
Anticipating Consequences	Identifying Big and Small Problems
Critical Thinking	Learning from Conflict
Identifying Reactions	Mediators
Identifying Solutions	Evaluating Rules and Laws
Causes and Effects of Conflicts	

Name: _____ Date: _____

Focus on Self

Self-Awareness

Naming Emotions

Emotional reactions are normal. You might see or hear something that makes you feel a certain way. It might make you feel joy, sorrow, or something else. Knowing how you feel about something is a good thing. It can help you understand your emotions in a healthy way.

Directions: Draw at least two things that make you feel each emotion.

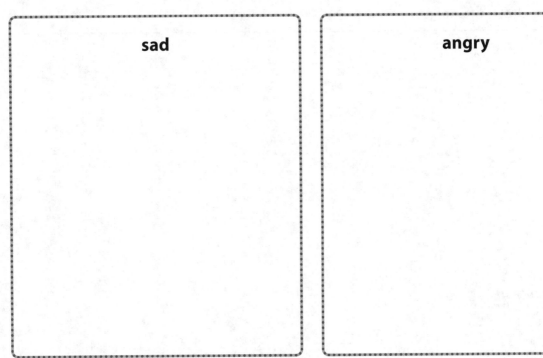

happy	proud
sad	angry

Name: _____ **Date:** _____

Using Self-Talk

Self-talk is a normal and healthy thing to do. You might use self-talk if you are worried about something. It can give you confidence. Self-talk is good for angry feelings, too. It can help calm you down so you can share your feelings with another person.

Directions: Draw a line to match each situation to helpful self-talk.

You forgot to study for your science test.	"I have practiced so many times, and I know I am ready."
Your dog is missing.	"I will talk to him and find out what happened before I react."
You burned the cookies you were baking.	"I will think about what I learned during class and do my best."
You are performing a song for your school.	"This was my first try. Next time, I will do better."
Your brother broke your favorite toy.	"Lots of people will help us. I'm sure she's safe."

Self-Management

Focus on Self

Name: _____ Date: _____

Body Language

People communicate with words. But they can also get a message across with their bodies. In fact, body language sometimes says things words don't. Pay attention to what someone is telling you with their body. It will help you know how they feel.

Directions: Write the emotion each person is feeling, based only on their body language.

1.

_____

3.

_____

2.

_____

4.

_____

Focus on Self

Social Awareness

Name: _____ Date: _____

Gestures

A gesture is a movement of the head or hand that communicates meaning. People use gestures often. They might use them while speaking to emphasize what they are saying. They might also use gestures without speaking. It's a way to get an idea across without saying a word.

Directions: Draw or describe a gesture to communicate each idea.

Yes.	No.
Wait.	Come here.
Hurry up.	I don't know.

Focus on Self
Relationship Skills

Name: _____ Date: _____

Focus on Self

Responsible Decision-Making

Recognizing Problems

People run into problems every day, so knowing how to solve them is important. It's also important to judge the size of a problem. Some problems are small, and you can handle them on your own. Others are big, and you should ask an adult for help.

Directions: Read the different problems you may have when cleaning your room. Circle whether they are big or small problems. Explain your reasoning.

1. Your favorite shirt is ripped.

big problem   small problem

_____

_____

2. A toy needs new batteries.

big problem   small problem

_____

_____

3. You can't find the lid to the toy bin.

big problem   small problem

_____

_____

4. A mirror has broken into many pieces.

big problem   small problem

_____

_____

Name: _____ **Date:** _____

Your Culture

Many things make up your family's culture. The language you speak and the way you dress are part of your culture. So are your religion or traditions. Your culture is something to celebrate. It is part of what makes you special.

Directions: Draw something about your family's culture. Then, explain your drawing.

_____

_____

_____

Name: _____ Date: _____

Helping Others

Helping others is important. It shows you care, and it feels good to do the right thing. Your family could probably use your help. You could help a sibling with homework or do a chore to help a parent. You might even reach out and talk to a lonely family member.

Directions: List three people in your family, and write one specific way you could help each of them. Then, draw yourself helping one of those family members.

1. _____

_____

2. _____

_____

3. _____

_____

Focus on Family

Self-Management

Name: _____ **Date:** _____

Showing Gratitude

Families often take care of each other. They show kindness and help out. They might give gifts or spend time together. You can probably think of some way a person in your family has taken care of you. When this happens, you should show gratitude. You can say something nice to show gratitude. You can also write a thank you note.

Directions: Write a thank you note to someone in your family who has taken care of you.

Date _____

Dear _____,

_____

_____

_____

_____

_____

_____

_____

_____

_____

_____

_____

Focus on Family
Social Awareness

Name: _____ Date: _____

Practicing Teamwork

A family is like a team. They are a group of people who work together to accomplish tasks. The members might not always get along, and there will be ups and downs. But they want to solve problems and support one another.

Directions: Read the story, and answer the questions.

Family Donations

The donation truck was coming tomorrow, and Aniyah's family had not even started collecting things. Her dad declared that Sunday was donation day. Aniyah felt a little overwhelmed. There was so much stuff to go through!

Her mom brought a big box into the room Aniyah and her little sister shared. Shae, her sister, started going through their stuffed animals. Aniyah began sorting the books and games. Before long, they had filled the box. Their room looked much more organized.

"Are you two finished?" her dad asked. His forehead was sweaty, and he was already carrying a box. "Just put that one on top of this one," he said. Aniyah and her sister lifted it onto the other box their dad held. He left to stack them by the front door.

In the kitchen, her mom was sorting cookbooks and serving trays. "How did we get so much stuff?" she wondered out loud. She put two cookbooks back in the cupboard and added three to a donation box.

Aniyah grinned. Donating will help her family and others!

1. How is Aniyah's family working as a team?

_____

_____

2. How will donating help her family and others?

_____

_____

Name: _____ **Date:** _____

Trying New Things

Your family probably has a lot of favorite things. There are meals you love to eat, shows you like to watch on TV, and games you like to play. But there are so many things in the world. Perhaps your family could try some new things. It's fun and adventurous, and you might discover some new things you all enjoy.

Directions: Write some of your family's favorite things. Then, brainstorm some new things you could try together.

	Your Family's Favorite	New One to Try
food or meal		
TV show or movie		
game		
activity to do together		

Name: _____ Date: _____

Growth Mindset

Everyone has strengths and weaknesses. Some of your skills might come easily to you. Others you may have had to work very hard to learn. When skills don't come easily, it is important to have a growth mindset. That means you believe you can get better at things through practice and hard work.

Directions: Put a star by the topics you already know a lot about or are good at doing. Write three topics or skills you would like to improve. Then, on another sheet of paper, write a plan to help you improve those things.

animals	painting	space
dividing	playing an instrument	speaking another language
drawing	playing a sport	spelling
fractions	reading	U.S. history
geography	research	world history
multiplying	singing	writing

1. _____

2. _____

3. _____

Focus on School   Self-Awareness

Name: _____ Date: _____

Managing Stress

Stress is an emotion people can feel at any age. You might feel stressed if you have a lot of activities. Or you may feel stressed if you have an argument with a loved one. Sometimes, school and learning might make you feel stressed, too. Deep-breathing techniques can help you feel better in a stressful moment.

Directions: Follow the steps for a deep-breathing exercise. Then, answer the questions.

 Step 1: If possible, sit in a comfortable position.

 Step 2: Breathe in deeply through your nose as you count to four.

 Step 3: Hold your breath for four seconds.

 Step 4: Purse your lips as though you are whistling. Exhale slowly through your mouth as you count to four.

 Step 5: Repeat at least four times.

1. How do you feel after doing the deep-breathing exercise?

   _____

   _____

2. Write about a time you felt stressed. How did your body feel? How would this exercise help next time?

   _____

   _____

   _____

   _____

Focus on School

Self-Management

Name: _____ Date: _____

Understanding Different Rules

Rules are necessary. They help keep people safe. Different places all have their own rules. That can make it confusing to remember which set of rules to follow. Understanding why places have different rules is helpful.

Directions: Fill in the letter that shows the best place for each rule.

1. Walk in a straight line.

    Ⓐ classroom   Ⓑ playground   Ⓒ cafeteria   Ⓓ hallway

2. Raise your hand before you speak.

    Ⓐ classroom   Ⓑ playground   Ⓒ cafeteria   Ⓓ hallway

3. Take turns on the equipment.

    Ⓐ classroom   Ⓑ playground   Ⓒ cafeteria   Ⓓ hallway

4. Finish your work.

    Ⓐ classroom   Ⓑ playground   Ⓒ cafeteria   Ⓓ hallway

5. Do not share food.

    Ⓐ classroom   Ⓑ playground   Ⓒ cafeteria   Ⓓ hallway

Name: _____ **Date:** _____

Resolving Conflicts

Conflicts are part of life. Resolving conflicts is an important skill. There are different kinds of outcomes when you solve a conflict. *Win-win* means both people are happy with the way the problem was solved. *Win-lose* means one person is happy, but the other is not. *Lose-lose* means neither person is happy with the outcome.

Directions: Read the story. Label each solution to the problem as *win-win*, *win-lose*, or *lose-lose*.

The Popular Book

Shawn and Manuel both love to read. The librarian, Mr. Sachs, showed their class a few new books he was adding to the shelves. Both Shawn and Manuel thought the book about starting a colony on Mars sounded amazing. When Mr. Sachs was finished talking, they both went up to him.

"Can I borrow that book?" the boys said in unison.

The librarian looked troubled and said, "We only have one copy."

Shawn and Manuel looked at each other. Now what?

1. Mr. Sachs gives each boy a different book. Shawn's is about comets, and Manuel's is about the moon.

   _____

2. Mr. Sachs lets Manuel check out the book and tells Shawn he can have it later.

   _____

3. Mr. Sachs tells the boys he will get an extra copy, and they can both check out the book tomorrow.

   _____

Focus on School

Relationship Skills

Name: _____ Date: _____

Focus on School

Responsible Decision-Making

Making Good Decisions

You will need to make a lot of important decisions in your life. There are things you can do to help you make good decisions. Before you make a choice, look at all the options, and think about how each choice matches up with what you want or need. You should also look at the facts about each choice. Remember, sometimes there isn't a right or wrong choice. You just have to make the one that is best for you.

Directions: Look at the posters of two candidates running for class president. Then, answer the question.

Candidate A	**Candidate B**

If I am elected, I will:

- have the cafeteria serve pizza every Friday.

- make sure our library has the newest books.

- begin an outdoor education classroom.

If I am elected, I will:

- have the cafeteria serve smoothies every Friday.

- make sure our playground has new recess equipment.

- begin a weekly school news broadcast.

1. Who would you vote for? Why?

_____

_____

_____

Name: _____ Date: _____

Integrity

Having integrity means being honest and fair. It means you do the right thing, even when no one is watching. Integrity is a good character trait to have. You can treat others with kindness and be fair when playing with others. You can be honest, even when it is hard. If you look, you will find lots of chances to show integrity.

Directions: Look at the image, and write at least three ways you could show integrity and help.

1. _____

_____

2. _____

_____

3. _____

_____

Name: _____ Date: _____

Setting Goals

A community can be a big, busy place. There are many people and activities. If a community needs to change in some way, it is helpful for people to work together. They can set a goal to buy, repair, or create something. To accomplish that goal, the people will need to brainstorm ideas. They might need to assign jobs. They will certainly need teamwork.

Directions: Read the story, and answer the questions.

Cole County Clock

The clock tower has been in front of the courthouse in Cole County for almost 100 years. The people in the community are proud of its beauty and history. But it is in need of repairs. The clock is dirty and worn, and it does not keep accurate time. The tower is not very stable anymore either. A small group of people have formed a committee with one goal: fix the clock tower. But they are not sure how to accomplish their goal. They know it will take a lot of help and a lot of money.

1. How could the committee raise money? Give at least two suggestions.

_____

_____

_____

_____

2. What types of volunteer jobs could help repair the clock?

_____

_____

_____

3. Why does the community want to save the clock tower?

_____

_____

Name: _____ **Date:** _____

Noticing Needs

Your community has many interesting places. It might have homes, parks, stores, and roads. You might attend school or worship there, and you may have neighbors and friends. In every community, there are things that need to be done and ways people can help. No matter your age or skill level, there are ways you can help.

Directions: Draw one way you can help your community. Then, explain your drawing.

```




```

_____

_____

_____

Name: _____ Date: _____

Focus on Community

Relationship Skills

Leadership

Communities need all types of leaders. Some lead the government, such as a mayor or council member. Others, such as principals and business owners, lead schools or businesses. Leaders don't all look or act the same. They have different goals and tasks. But all leaders work with others to get things done.

Directions: Read the story, and answer the questions.

Save the Ducks

Miss Silver was a quiet woman who lived by herself. Every day, she walked to the park, sat by the pond, and fed the ducks. One day, she noticed construction workers setting up cones along the pond. They were going to drain the pond to make room for a playground.

Miss Silver got to work. Someone needed to save the ducks. She called the mayor and left a voicemail. She talked to a few of her friends and interviewed parents who wanted the playground. She presented all her findings to the town council, and they agreed. The community decided to keep the pond.

1. How is Miss Silver a leader?

_____

_____

2. What traits do you think a good leader should have?

_____

_____

3. Describe a time you were a leader.

_____

_____

_____

_____

Name: _____ Date: _____

Anticipating Consequences

Every action has consequences. If you lose a library book, you might have to pay to replace it. If you return a lost wallet, you might get a reward. These consequences are personal. They only affect one person. Some consequences are bigger. They can affect a whole community. Thinking about this will help you make good choices that can impact others.

Directions: Look at each image. Write the possible consequences for the community.

1.  _____
   _____
   _____
   _____
   _____
   _____

2.  _____
   _____
   _____
   _____
   _____
   _____
   _____

Focus on Community

Responsible Decision-Making

Name: _____ Date: _____

Focus on State

Self-Awareness

Advocating for Yourself

Your state government provides services for the people who live there. One of these services is public education. Money from the state can pay for things students need. But there are also things students want. No matter where you learn, there are things you need and want in order to help you learn. Knowing how to ask for these things can help you feel empowered. Sometimes, the answer might be no, but speaking up for yourself is still important.

Directions: Make a list of things students need and a list of things students might want. Then, answer the questions.

Students Need	Students Want
• _____	• _____
• _____	• _____
• _____	• _____
• _____	• _____
• _____	• _____

1. Imagine you do not have something you need for learning. Who would you talk to? What would you say?

   _____

   _____

   _____

2. What might happen if you do not speak up for yourself when you are trying to learn?

   _____

   _____

   _____

Name: _____ Date: _____

Helping Others

Sometimes, people need help from their states. A family might have trouble buying enough food. The state has programs to help them. A natural disaster might cause damage to a city. The state can help by giving money and sending people to clean up and serve. You may not be able to do as much as your state, but you can still help others.

Directions: Write at least two ways you could help each person.

Family Member

_____
_____
_____
_____
_____
_____

Friend

_____
_____
_____
_____
_____
_____

Neighbor

_____
_____
_____
_____
_____

Stranger

_____
_____
_____
_____
_____

Name: _____ Date: _____

Focus on State

Social Awareness

Identifying Just and Unjust Rules

You are probably expected to follow rules at home. You must also follow state laws. The laws help keep people and places safe. Laws should be just, which means they are fair. If an unjust law is made, people can work to change or get rid of the law. This has happened many times in history. In fact, it still happens today. Thinking about the fairness of rules and laws will help you to be more responsible.

Directions: Each of these laws has been true at one point or another. Circle whether each law was just or unjust, and explain why. Then, answer the questions.

just   unjust

1. Only white men can own property.

just   unjust

2. It is illegal for very small children to be left home alone.

just   unjust

3. Married women cannot open their own bank accounts.

just   unjust

4. Voters must have a job.

just   unjust

5. A driver can get a ticket for driving too slowly.

6. What rule in your home, school, or community do you think is unjust? Why?

_____

_____

7. What could you do to try and change the unjust rule?

_____

_____

_____

_____

Name: _____ **Date:** _____

Appreciating Cultures

States are full of people who are different. They speak different languages. They celebrate different holidays. They practice different religions. They have different cultures. Each culture is special. Each one has value. It can be fun to learn about them, and it is important to respect them.

Directions: Read the text about Chinatowns. Draw what you would like to do in a Chinatown. Then, explain your drawing.

Chinatowns

Many people from China moved to the United States in the 1800s. They mined for gold. They helped build railroads. Over the years, more people came from China to start new lives. But they did not want to forget their culture. Chinese immigrants often lived near each other in large cities. These areas became Chinatowns. These are neighborhoods where people from China came together to keep their culture alive. There are Chinatowns in many states. California and New York have the largest ones. Illinois, Hawai'i and Washington, DC, also have them.

A Chinatown is full of markets and small shops. They sell food, souvenirs, and other items. There are also many restaurants that serve delicious foods. Many people love to visit Chinatowns.

_____

_____

_____

Name: _____ Date: _____

Using Critical-Thinking Skills

Voters elect people to run the government in their states. When problems come up, people depend on those officials to help solve them. You need to be able to solve problems, too. Sometimes, your problems will be so big that you may need your state to help you. Thinking of solutions and carrying them out is important.

Directions: Write and draw about a time you faced a problem. Explain what the problem was and how you solved it.

_____

_____

_____

_____

_____

_____

_____

Name: _____ Date: _____

Discovering Personal Identity

Understanding who you are is important. You can think about what you like to do and what things matter most to you. You can reflect on your strengths and weaknesses. It is helpful to think about yourself in an honest and positive way. This is called a healthy self-image.

Directions: Complete the web with words or phrases that describe you.

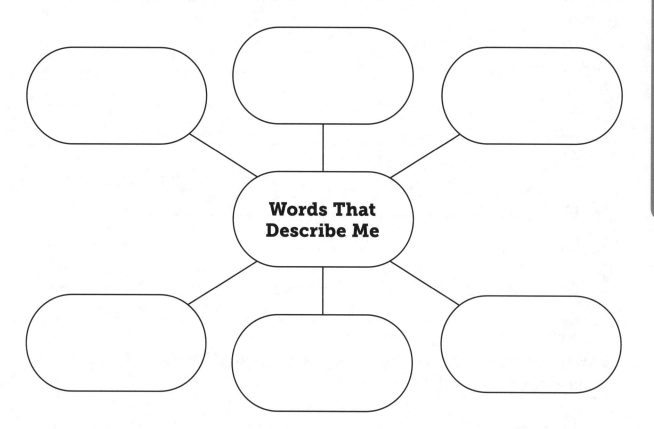

Words That Describe Me

Name: _____   Date: _____

Focus on Self

Self-Management

Understanding Feelings

There are many different types of feelings. Sometimes, you can feel emotions in your body. For example, if your favorite song comes on the radio, you might feel happy. You might feel it in your feet because you can't help tapping your toes. If you are nervous, you might feel sick to your stomach.

Directions: Describe how each emotion might feel in your body. Then, answer the prompt.

1. excited _____

_____

2. angry _____

_____

3. anxious _____

_____

4. sad _____

_____

5. Hurt is a feeling that can be emotional or physical. Explain why this is true. Include examples.

_____

_____

_____

_____

_____

Name: _____ Date: _____

Taking Others' Perspectives

You probably know that your emotions can affect how you act. But do you ever think about how your behavior might affect someone else's feelings? The way you feel can change the way you act. And then, the way you act can change how someone else feels. It's like a domino effect.

Directions: Read each scenario. Write how each person's behavior might affect someone else's emotions.

1. Addison is in such a good mood today. As she comes downstairs for breakfast, she volunteers to feed the dog, even though it is her sister's turn. How might this make her sister feel?

   _____

   _____

2. Dwane missed a lot of questions on his math quiz, and he is feeling really grouchy. At recess, his friend asks him to play soccer with her. He just scowls and walks away. How might this make Dwane's friend feel?

   _____

   _____

3. Rubi watched a scary show last night and can't stop thinking about it. At lunch, she tells her little brother all about what she saw. How might this make her brother feel?

   _____

   _____

4. Maurice is so proud of his new bike. When he shows it to his neighbor, he can't help telling him about its special features and how much it cost. How might this make his neighbor feel?

   _____

   _____

Social Awareness

Focus on Self

Name: _____ **Date:** _____

Focus on Self

Relationship Skills

Seeking Support

Sometimes, you will need help. For example, you might have a problem that someone can help you fix. But other times, you will need support, which is different. You might feel sad, alone, stressed, or worried. You don't need anyone to fix your problem. You just need someone to encourage you or listen. You can ask a trusted adult or friend for support when you need it.

Directions: Draw a time you received support from someone. Then, explain your drawing.

_____

_____

_____

Name: _____ Date: _____

Identifying Reactions

People have reactions to news and events. Depending on how the information makes them feel, they will respond in different ways. When you find out some news, stop and think about how you should react. Is it something really big or important? Or is it something that isn't a big deal? Appropriate reactions will help keep your feelings in control.

Directions: Describe the reaction you might have to each event.

1. You learn your family is leaving tomorrow for a vacation.

   _____

   _____

2. Your sister eats the piece of cake you were saving for yourself.

   _____

   _____

3. Your favorite relative is coming for a weeklong visit.

   _____

   _____

4. Your brother helps you understand a tricky math problem.

   _____

   _____

Name: _____ Date: _____

Developing Interests

Think about your neighborhood. Your home is there, and you might have neighbors or a local park, store, or school within walking distance. There may also be sidewalks and stop signs or traffic lights. Your neighborhood may also have things to do outside or with friends. You spend a lot of time in your neighborhood, so finding fun things to do is helpful.

Directions: Answer the questions about your neighborhood.

1. Write at least four things people can do in your neighborhood.

   • _____

   • _____

   • _____

   • _____

2. What is your favorite thing to do in your neighborhood?

   _____

   _____

3. Write two new things you are interested in doing in your neighborhood.

   • _____

   • _____

Name: _____ Date: _____

Overcoming Fear

Trying something new takes courage. A person might be afraid they will fail or get hurt, or they might worry that something will take too long to learn. But overcoming fear in order to try new things is very important. If you want to try something new, don't let fear of the unknown get you down. Be brave, and go for it. It might take time and practice, but it will be worth it.

Directions: Read the story, and answer the questions.

The Bike Ride

Will was so excited to get his new bike last summer, but it has been sitting in the garage for months. His dad volunteered to help him many times, but Will always made an excuse. He would never be able to ride as well as the neighborhood kids.

One day, there was a knock at the door. Will was surprised to see his neighbor, Antony, on his porch. "Grab your bike, Will," Antony said. "Let's walk them to the empty lot and practice riding."

Will wasn't sure what to say. Antony must know Will couldn't ride, and he was offering to help. Will grinned and went to get his helmet and bike. He was still nervous, but if Antony was willing to help, Will wanted to try.

1. Why is Will afraid to ride his bike?

_____

_____

2. Why does he want to try to practice with Antony?

_____

_____

3. What is something you were afraid to try? What happened when you tried it?

_____

_____

Name: _____ Date: _____

Focus on Neighborhood
Social Awareness

Recognizing Others' Strengths

There are so many different types of people in the world. They have varied talents, gifts, and interests. This is true of the people in your neighborhood, too. Noticing what others are good at will help you appreciate them. Giving compliments or saying thank you will make them feel special.

Directions: Draw two pictures of neighbors doing something they are good at, and explain each drawing.

_____

_____

_____

_____

_____

Communicating Effectively

There are many things that help neighbors communicate effectively. For example, when two people talk, they each have a job. One is the sender, and one is the receiver. The sender is the one doing the talking. The receiver is the one listening. In a good conversation, they switch jobs often. When they each do their jobs well, their communication is clear.

Directions: Write how each person should do their job when communicating.

sender   receiver

Focus on Neighborhood
Relationship Skills

Sender

• eyes: _____

• mouth: _____

• other: _____

Receiver

• eyes: _____

• ears: _____

• other: _____

Identifying Solutions

Conflict is a natural part of living in a neighborhood. All people cannot agree all the time. This is why knowing how to solve a conflict is so important. Learn about the problem, think of solutions, and then choose one. These are basic steps to ending a conflict.

Directions: Read the story, and answer the questions.

The New Neighbor

The Aldens had lived in their house for a long time. When the Pruett family moved next door, the Aldens brought them cookies. They talked for a bit, and both families were pleased to meet each other.

Mr. Pruett often parked his car in front of the Aldens' house. Within a few weeks, the Aldens noticed a problem. They were not getting their mail when Mr. Pruett's car was parked out front because it was blocking their mailbox. Mr. Alden talked to Mr. Pruett about it. Both men were unhappy. Mr. Alden wanted his mail, and Mr. Pruett wanted a place to park.

1. What is the problem in the story?

_____

_____

2. What are two possible solutions?

_____

_____

3. Draw one of your solutions.

Name: _____ Date: _____

Integrating Social Identity

People see themselves a certain way. You have thoughts about your traits, what you are good at, and what you would like to learn more about. It can be very helpful to think about how others see you, too. Your friends spend time with you, and they know you well. Knowing how they see you can help you realize the image you show to others. It can also allow you to see yourself in a different way.

Directions: Answer the questions about yourself. Ask a friend the questions, and record their answers. Then, answer the last question.

Focus on Friends

Self-Awareness

Your Answers	**Your Friend's Answers**
1. What three adjectives would you use to describe yourself?	**4.** What three adjectives would you use to describe me?
_____	_____
_____	_____
_____	_____
2. What is something you are good at?	**5.** What is something I am good at?
_____	_____
3. What do you like about yourself?	**6.** What do you like about me?
_____	_____

7. Do you think your friend sees you the way you see yourself? Explain your answer.

_____

_____

_____

_____

Name: _____ Date: _____

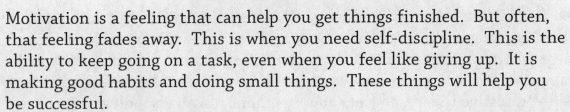

Exhibiting Self-Discipline

Motivation is a feeling that can help you get things finished. But often, that feeling fades away. This is when you need self-discipline. This is the ability to keep going on a task, even when you feel like giving up. It is making good habits and doing small things. These things will help you be successful.

Directions: Read the story, and answer the questions.

Running the Race

Charles was supposed to meet his friend, Jamie, before school. They were training to run in a race at school. Charles slept in and arrived late to meet her. Jamie was already warmed up by the time Charles arrived.

"I don't feel like running today," Charles complained. "I just can't stay motivated to practice."

"It is hard to get up so early," Jamie agreed. "But I make sure to go to bed a little earlier on nights before we practice. I lay out my running clothes, and I make sure I have the ingredients for a healthy breakfast."

"Wow!" Charles said. "That's impressive."

1. Which friend has self-discipline? Give an example to show how you know.

_____

_____

2. How did Charles's lack of self-discipline affect Jamie?

_____

_____

3. Which friend do you think you are most like? Why?

_____

_____

Name: _____   **Date:** _____

Showing Concern for Others

You interact with people every day, especially friends. Occasionally, you might notice that a friend feels sad or scared. Showing concern for that person is a kind thing to do. You could talk to them or offer to get help. A smile or hug can also help a friend feel a lot better.

Directions: Read the story, and answer the questions.

A Helping Hand

Norah spent a lot of time at her best friend Zoe's house. Zoe's grandmother lived with her and her mom. One day, her grandmother fell and broke her hip. Norah knew Zoe was worried and scared, so she talked to her mom about what they could do to help. Her mom suggested they bring the family dinner.

They dropped the food off a few hours later. Zoe and her mom had just arrived home from the hospital and were very grateful for the delicious dinner.

"Grandma is going to have surgery tomorrow," Zoe told Norah. "My mom and I are going to wait at the hospital all day. I want to be there, but it's going to be a long, boring day."

Norah had a great idea. She would get started on it as soon as she got home.

1. How did Norah and her mom show concern for Zoe and her mom?

_____

2. What do you think Norah's great idea was?

_____

_____

3. Describe a time when you showed concern for someone.

_____

_____

Name: _____ Date: _____

Focus on Friends
Relationship Skills

Leadership

Good leaders are honest and brave. They listen to others and are team players. Leaders also influence other people. They may have a great idea or want to make a change, so they will share information to persuade others. If you want to be a leader and influence others, you can find out what they want or need. Research to find out more about the topic, and decide what you think about it. Then, share what you learned with your friends. You might influence their thoughts about an issue.

Directions: The president of the student council wants to make a change at school. Read the petition, and answer the questions.

Petition for Water Bottle Fillers

Our water fountains need to be replaced. The new ones should also be equipped with a spout for refilling water bottles. Here are the reasons why:

1. It is cleaner. People put their mouths on regular water fountains. This does not happen when they fill their water bottles.

2. It conserves water. Water fountains waste water because people don't drink all the water that comes out. All the water from the filler goes right into a water bottle.

3. It keeps students in class. Thirsty students ask to leave class to get a drink. But they can keep their water bottles in class so they won't have to leave.

Sign the petition so the school will install water bottle fillers!

1. How does the president of the student council try to influence people?

_____

_____

2. Would you sign this petition? Why or why not?

_____

_____

Name: _____ **Date:** _____

Causes and Effects of Conflicts

Conflicts happen to everyone, even friends. Every conflict has a cause and an effect. The cause is the reason why the conflict happened. The effect is what happened because of the conflict. Figuring out the cause and effect of a conflict can help you understand it. And understanding a conflict can help you solve it. That can help you be a better friend.

Directions: Read the causes for different conflicts between friends. Draw or write about the possible effects of the conflicts.

1. **Cause:** Jack and his friend are playing a video game. His friend has been playing for several minutes and will not give Jack a turn.

   Effect

2. **Cause:** Akshar and his friend are racing at recess. Akshar trips and falls, and his friend laughs at him.

   Effect

3. **Cause:** Macie told her friend some private information. Her friend told a few other classmates.

   Effect

Name: _____ Date: _____

Core Values

Your core values are the things that are most important to you. They make you who you are. Honesty and kindness are examples of core values. Knowing your core values can guide you in your everyday life. They can help you know what to do or how to respond to situations in your community.

Directions: Circle three core values that are important to you. Complete the boxes by explaining how you could use those core values to help your community.

adventurous	friendly	intelligent	open-minded
dependable	hardworking	kind	responsible
faithful	honest	loyal	trustworthy

Core Value: _____

_____

_____

Core Value: _____

_____

_____

Core Value: _____

_____

_____

Name: _____ Date: _____

Trying New Things

It can be intimidating to try new things. You might be afraid something will be too hard or you won't do well. But there are so many benefits to trying something new. You might find a new hobby or passion. You might learn a new skill that could come in handy later. You might even meet new people in your community and learn new ways to help others. It can be worth it to take a risk and try something new.

Directions: Read the story, and answer the questions.

Cooking Class

When his mom got a new full-time job, Drew knew he would have more responsibilities at home. His mom would get home late in the afternoon and would probably be tired after a hard day's work. Drew decided to learn to cook so he could make dinner sometimes.

He signed up for a class called Easy Dinners at the community center. He was nervous because he had never cooked. But his teacher was kind and patient.

Drew's workspace was next to a man named Mr. Tareen. Mr. Tareen helped Drew practice his knife skills. Other people in the class shared tips with Drew, too.

A few weeks later, he made meatloaf and mashed potatoes for dinner. His mom was impressed and grateful. Drew couldn't wait to go back to his cooking class and learn more.

1. Why does Drew decide to learn something new?

_____

_____

2. How could Drew use his new skill in his community?

_____

_____

_____

Name: _____ Date: _____

Taking Others' Perspectives

Most of the time, it is easy to understand other people's reactions. Other times, you might need to think about things from their perspectives. This means you try to think about something the way someone else does. You might consider what you know about that person or the situation. This can help you identify how someone else is feeling.

Directions: Read the story. Then, describe how the next part of the story will feel from each person's perspective.

The Shaggy Pup

The community animal shelter had a new stray. It was a black shaggy puppy with no collar. Ms. Pérez was looking for a new dog and fell in love with the shaggy pup. She filled out an application to adopt her and made plans to bring the dog home the next day.

In the morning, a frantic man came into the shelter. "My puppy has been missing for two days!" he exclaimed. "I've been looking everywhere. Is there any way she ended up here?"

The shelter director talked to the man. He asked for a description of the missing dog. The shaggy puppy was definitely his. Just then, Ms. Pérez came in. The director sighed. He was going to have to explain the situation to the man and Ms. Pérez.

1. shelter director: _____

_____

2. dog owner: _____

_____

3. Ms. Pérez: _____

_____

Name: _____ Date: _____

Communicating Effectively

Listening is different from hearing. When a person is speaking to you, it's your job to listen. Being an active listener is especially important. This means you concentrate on what the other person is saying. You ask questions if you don't understand something. You might even nod your head to let the speaker know you are paying attention. Being an active listener helps you learn better. It shows respect to the speaker.

Directions: Imagine you are listening to a person in your community give an important speech. They are speaking in the middle of a busy park. Complete the web to show how you can be an active listener.

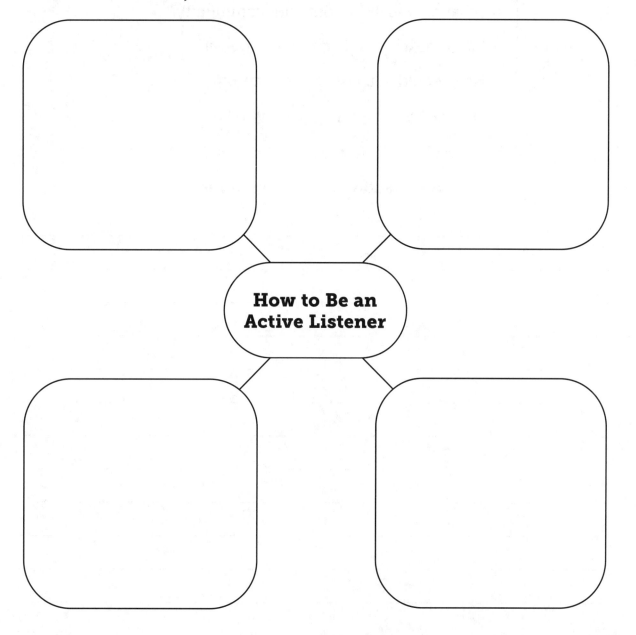

Focus on Community
Relationship Skills

Name: _____ Date: _____

Focus on Community

Responsible Decision-Making

Reflecting on Your Community

Reflecting is an important part of understanding things. You can reflect on your relationships with others. You can think about what you are learning. You can make goals for the future. You can also reflect on your community. Doing this will help you know what parts you are thankful for and which parts you would like to help change.

Directions: Use the questions to help you write a paragraph reflecting on your community.

- What do you like about your community?

- What makes your community special?

- How would you change your community?

- How can you help your community?

A Reflection on My Community

_____

_____

_____

_____

_____

_____

_____

_____

_____

_____

Name: _____ **Date:** _____

Developing Interests

Each state is different and unique. Some are known for their beaches, while others have spectacular mountains. They might have national parks or bustling cities. There are special things about where you live, too. It can be fun to find things to do in your state.

Directions: Answer the questions about your state.

1. In which state do you live? _____

2. What is special about your state?

_____

_____

3. Draw yourself doing something in your state that you enjoy.

Name: _____ Date: _____

Focus on State

Self-Management

Using Calendars

Using a calendar is a great way to stay organized. It can help all kinds of people. A student might note when homework is due. Families can keep track of their schedules. Businesses use them to schedule meetings. Calendars are also used by state officials. They can help people plan and carry out important events.

Directions: Your state is celebrating a milestone birthday. Study the calendar of events. Then, answer the questions.

Monday	9:00 a.m.: governor arrives 10:30 a.m.: set up lunch buffet 12:00 p.m.: lunch is served
Tuesday	8:00 a.m.: birthday event planners do TV interview 5:30 p.m.: governor gives speech
Wednesday	12:00 p.m.: students read state essays 7:00 p.m.: state residents share memories
Thursday	4:00 p.m.: state history film is played
Friday	6:00 p.m.: birthday party begins in Capitol Park 9:00 p.m.: fireworks begin
Saturday	10:00 a.m.: birthday parade begins downtown 1:00 p.m.: clean-up crew begins work

1. What happens on Friday at 9:00 p.m.? _____

2. At which two events could you listen to others speak? _____

_____

3. Which event would you most like to attend? Why? _____

_____

4. What event would you like to add to the week? Why? _____

_____

Name: _____ Date: _____

Expressing Gratitude

There are many different ways to show your gratitude. You can use words. You can write a note. You can send a message or email. You can even say thank you in another language. Over 350 different languages are spoken in the United States. Many of them are likely spoken in your state. That's a lot of ways to express gratitude!

Directions: Research four languages that are spoken in your state, not including the one you speak most often. Write the names of the languages on the lines in each cloud. Write how to say *thank you* in those languages in colorful, creative ways.

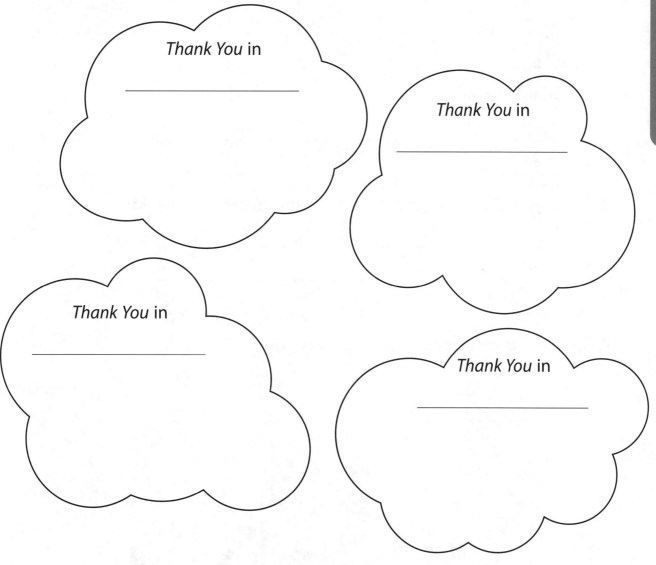

Thank You in

_____

Thank You in

_____

Thank You in

_____

Thank You in

_____

Focus on State

Social Awareness

Name: _____ Date: _____

Practicing Teamwork

Teamwork happens everywhere. Students, employees, and families all have to work as teams. People in state governments also use teamwork. They might have different ideas about how to solve problems. But they often have common goals. When you're on a team, you should do your share. When everyone does part of the work, your team can be more successful.

Focus on State

Relationship Skills

Directions: Answer the questions.

1. Describe a time you worked with others as a team. What was the goal? Your team might have been with family, classmates, or a sports team.

   _____

   _____

2. What did you do to help?

   _____

   _____

3. Who were the other people on the team? What did they do?

   _____

   _____

   _____

4. Did your team meet the goal? Why or why not?

   _____

   _____

   _____

Name: _____ Date: _____

Evaluating Impact

Imagine throwing a rock into a pond. That rock makes small ripples, and those ripples make larger ripples. The effects are still there, long after the rock is gone. Life is like ripples in a pond because people and events affect others' lives. A new state law can ripple out and affect your life.

Directions: Read each situation. Write how it might affect your life.

1. Your state passes a law that homes must use solar energy.

   _____

   _____

2. Your school passes a new rule that all students must ride a bus to and from school.

   _____

   _____

3. Your family decides that no one can watch TV after dinner.

   _____

   _____

4. Your state passes a law that no one under 12 years old can use the internet.

   _____

   _____

Responsible Decision-Making

Focus on State

Name: _____ Date: _____

Focus on Self

Self-Awareness

Understanding Emotional Intensity

Imagine a summer day. The sun is bright, and sweat is beading on your forehead. Now, imagine an oven. It is turned up so it can bake cookies. Both are hot, but they are not the same intensity. Intensity is the degree to which something happens. Your feelings can have different intensities, too. Recognizing this will help you express your emotions in a way that makes sense.

Directions: Write an emotion. Then, follow the prompts.

Emotion: _____

1. Describe a time when have you felt this emotion at a high intensity.

_____

_____

_____

2. Describe a time when have you felt this emotion at a low intensity.

_____

_____

_____

3. Draw what this emotion looks like at a high intensity and a low intensity.

High Intensity	**Low Intensity**

Name: _____ Date: _____

Stress-Management Strategies

Feeling a little stress is normal. You might be busy with family, school, and friends. You might play a sport or an instrument, too. These things can take up time and energy, which can lead to stress. Sometimes, you might feel a lot of stress, but there are things you can do to manage those feelings, such as regular exercise. Getting your heart rate up for a few minutes is good for you.

Directions: Read the different types of exercises. Choose at least four, and create an exercise routine.

arm circles	lunges	run in place
burpees	mountain climbers	sit-ups
high knees	plank	squats
jumping jacks	pushups	wall sit

My Exercise Routine

Exercise: _____ How many or how long? _____

Exercise: _____ How many or how long? _____

Exercise: _____ How many or how long? _____

Exercise: _____ How many or how long? _____

Directions: Complete your routine, and then answer the questions.

1. How did you feel after exercising?

_____

_____

2. What makes you feel stressed? Describe how exercise could help.

_____

_____

_____

Name: _____ Date: _____

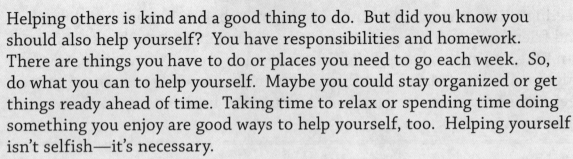

Helping Yourself

Helping others is kind and a good thing to do. But did you know you should also help yourself? You have responsibilities and homework. There are things you have to do or places you need to go each week. So, do what you can to help yourself. Maybe you could stay organized or get things ready ahead of time. Taking time to relax or spending time doing something you enjoy are good ways to help yourself, too. Helping yourself isn't selfish—it's necessary.

Focus on Self

Social Awareness

Directions: Draw one way you can help yourself this week. Then, describe your drawing.

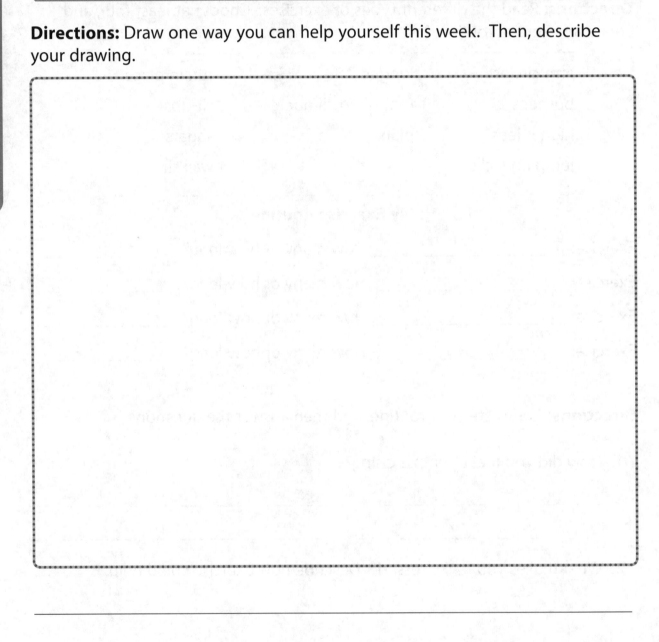

_____

_____

_____

Name: _____ Date: _____

Communicating Effectively

You communicate with others every day. Sometimes, you are the speaker. In other moments, you are the listener. As the listener, you have a responsibility. You should make sure you know what the other person is trying to tell you. You might paraphrase what they said. This means you put what they said into your own words. Paraphrasing can help you remember their ideas. Sometimes, what they said will not make sense to you. So, you might need to check for understanding.

Directions: Answer the questions.

1. What are two ways you can check for understanding when talking to a friend?

_____

_____

_____

2. Describe a time when paraphrasing would have been helpful.

_____

_____

_____

3. Listen to a classmate or family member describe their dream vacation. Paraphrase what they said. Include as many details as you can remember.

_____

_____

_____

_____

_____

Focus on Self
Relationship Skills

Name: _____ Date: _____

Focus on Self

Responsible Decision-Making

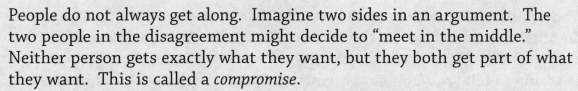

Compromise

People do not always get along. Imagine two sides in an argument. The two people in the disagreement might decide to "meet in the middle." Neither person gets exactly what they want, but they both get part of what they want. This is called a *compromise*.

Directions: Read the story, and answer the questions.

Dinner Compromise

Riley and Becca were hungry for dinner. When their dad said they were going out to eat, both girls were excited.

"I have been craving pizza!" Riley exclaimed. "We should go to Papa's Pizza."

Becca shook her head. "No, we should go to Amore's Italian. I love their spaghetti."

Their dad laughed. "Well, we can't go to both places. Can you two find a compromise?"

"We could go to Amore's Italian tonight and Papa's Pizza next time," Becca suggested.

"Or maybe we should go to Mario's," Riley said. "They have pizza and spaghetti."

1. Is Becca's idea a compromise? Why or why not?

_____

_____

2. Is Riley's idea a compromise? Why or why not?

_____

_____

3. Describe a time when you had to make a compromise.

_____

_____

Name: _____ Date: _____

Being Open-Minded

You might already know a lot of your favorite things. You might have a favorite movie, food, color, sport, hobby, or book. But don't be afraid to try new things. If you are looking for something new, you might not have to look further than your own family. They might have some favorites they would like to share with you.

Directions: List three family members, and write things they enjoy. Talk to them if you are unsure. Then, answer the questions.

1. _____ enjoys _____
_____

2. _____ enjoys _____
_____

3. _____ enjoys _____
_____

4. Which idea from the list would you like to try? Why?

_____

_____

_____

5. Describe how a family member can help you try new things.

_____

_____

_____

Focus on Family

Self-Awareness

Name: _____ Date: _____

Setting Goals

Families spend a lot of time together, and they often live in the same spaces. Sometimes, families make a goal that involves all members. The goal might be to eat healthier, work on a big project, or spend more time together. Working on a goal together can be fun. It divides up the work. It lets people have fun with each other.

Directions: Read the story, and answer the questions.

Garden Goal

Nyra's parents had a big project idea, and they wanted everyone's help.

"Why should we always have to go to the store for our vegetables?" her mother asked. "We should start a garden!"

Nyra's dad agreed. "Growing fresh vegetables means we'll spend less money, and we can spend time together outside."

"Actually, this sounds like a good idea," Nyra admitted. "But do we know how to start a garden?"

"Not yet!" her mom said cheerfully. "But our goal is to have a garden planted with four different types of seeds by the end of the month."

"That is a big goal. Do you have a plan?" Nyra asked.

"Of course we do!" Nyra's dad said, grinning. "Now, let's get to work!"

1. What is Nyra's family's goal? _____

_____

2. Do you think this is a realistic goal? Why or why not? _____

_____

3. What steps do you think the family might need to take to meet their goal?

_____

_____

Focus on Family

Self-Management

Name: _____ **Date:** _____

Connecting Feelings and Actions

You have learned that your feelings affect your actions. If you are angry, you are more likely to shout at a sibling. If you are happy, you are more likely to go with the flow. Other people do the same thing. If you observe a person's actions, you might be able to tell how they are feeling. Understanding how someone feels can help you get along with them.

Directions: Read about different people's actions. Describe how they might be feeling.

Action	Feeling
1. Maya comes home from school and throws her backpack on the floor. She goes straight to her room and slams the door.	
2. Devin was home alone. When his sister arrives home, he sits by her and asks her to tell him all about her day.	
3. Leila's dad gets home late from work. He says hello, but immediately heads to his home office and asks everyone to keep it down while he works.	
4. Renee's little sister comes skipping into the family room. She has a handful of candy and offers Renee a piece.	

Focus on Family

Social Awareness

Name: _____ Date: _____

Focus on Family

Relationship Skills

Developing Positive Relationships

One way to make a family relationship stronger is to find things you have in common. Maybe you and a family member enjoy the same music. Maybe you love the same sport. Finding things you have in common with a family member can help you get along. It can bring you closer together and make you feel good.

Directions: Think of a connection you have with a family member. It might be a special memory or something you both like to do. It could be an event you went to together or something you have in common. Draw the connection, and explain your drawing.

_____

_____

_____

Name: _____ **Date:** _____

Resolving Conflicts

You have likely had conflicts with people in your home. It might have been with a sibling or parent. Maybe it was with a guardian, grandparent, or cousin. You live with them and spend a lot of time together. So it's only natural you don't always get along. But when conflicts come, it is important to know how to resolve them.

Directions: Read the text. Follow the steps to help the family resolve the conflict.

Borrowed Compass

Isaiah let his brother, Evan, borrow his compass. Evan took it on a hike with friends. While they were out, Evan lost the compass. Isaiah is very upset.

Step 1: Identify the Problem

_____

_____

Step 2: Listen (Write each brother's perspective.)

_____

_____

_____

_____

Step 3: Think of Solutions

• _____

• _____

Step 4: Choose a Solution

_____

Name: _____ Date: _____

Focus on School

Self-Awareness

Personal Identity

How you see yourself is important to your identity. You can think about answers to questions to understand yourself better. Some questions might be about your character. Are you kind? Are you honest? Are you responsible? Other questions might help you figure out what kind of learner you are. These can be useful to you as a student.

Directions: Circle if you agree or disagree with each statement. Then, answer the prompt.

1. I learn best from listening to the teacher.   agree   disagree

2. I learn best from reading a book.   agree   disagree

3. I learn best from watching someone do a task.   agree   disagree

4. I like to complete work by myself.   agree   disagree

5. I like to complete work in a group.   agree   disagree

6. I work best when it is quiet.   agree   disagree

7. I work best when there is background noise.   agree   disagree

8. I like assignments with one right answer.   agree   disagree

9. I like assignments with a lot of possibilities.   agree   disagree

10. I catch on quickly.   agree   disagree

11. I need time to think about what I'm learning.   agree   disagree

12. Describe your ideal learning situation.

_____

_____

_____

_____

Name: _____ Date: _____

Using Checklists

There are many different strategies to stay organized. One way is to use a checklist. A list can be about anything. It can be a list of chores to do or things to buy at the store. Lists are especially helpful at school. Seeing a list can break down a big task into smaller pieces. And many people love the feeling of crossing things off their lists.

Directions: Study the list of things Jenna needs and wants to do at school today. Then, answer the questions.

To Do Today

- study spelling words

- read a chapter of a book

- feed the class hamster

- play soccer on the playground

- finish math homework

- play with friends

- make weekend plans

- answer history questions

1. Jenna wants to divide her list into two categories. What categories would you suggest?

_____

_____

2. Put stars by three items you think are most important on Jenna's list.

3. Do you think a checklist would help you? Why or why not?

_____

_____

Focus on School
Self-Management

Name: _____ Date: _____

Social Norms

Different places often need different rules. For example, a library and a baseball field do not have the same expectations. You spend part of your day learning. It may be in a school, home, or somewhere else. The rules you follow when you are learning are not the same as when you are playing. Knowing the rules of different places can help you act appropriately.

Directions: Think about the rules of the place where you learn. Then, think about the rules of another place you go. Complete the Venn diagram to compare the rules of both places. Write at least two ideas in each section.

Where I Learn

Both

_____

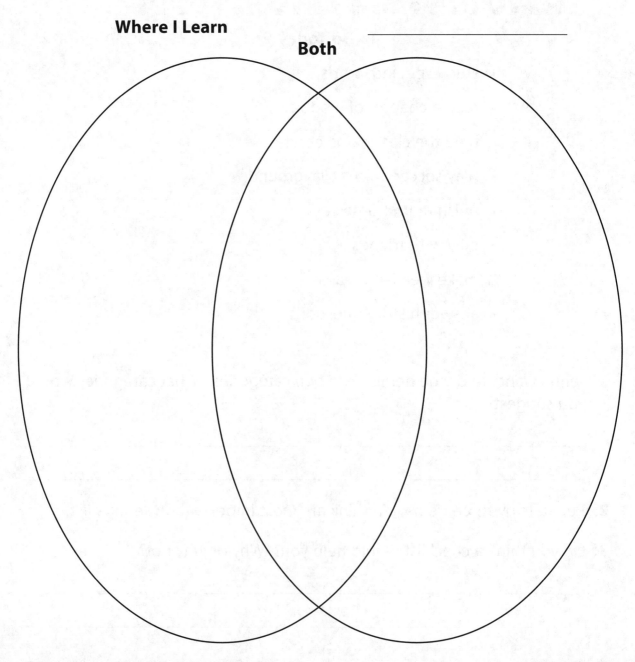

Name: _____ Date: _____

Standing Up for Others

All people have certain rights. Students have rights, too. They have the right to a fair and equal education, to learning materials, and to trained teachers. Sometimes, students do not get equal rights. You and other people can stand up for those students. You can talk to your teachers or classmates about making things fair. Your family might be able to help, too. Standing up for others feels good and is the right thing to do.

Directions: Read the story, and answer the questions.

The New Student

Tess was excited to see a new student sitting in her classroom on Monday morning. Miss Weiss introduced him as Javier, and he had just moved from Costa Rica.

"Javier speaks Spanish," Miss Weiss told the class. "He's learning English, but only speaks a little."

Over the next few days, Tess noticed that Javier worked with a tutor to practice English. She saw that Miss Weiss gave him work in both English and Spanish. She also noticed Javier didn't play with anyone at recess. Tess thought she knew why. No one in her class could speak Spanish. She decided to talk to the teacher about it.

"Javier has the right to have friends," she told Miss Weiss. "I think we should all learn to speak a little Spanish. Or maybe his tutor can help us talk to each other."

"Those are great ideas, Tess," Miss Weiss told her. "Let's figure out a plan."

1. In what way is Javier being treated fairly? Explain your answer.

_____

_____

2. How does Tess stand up for Javier?

_____

Name: _____ Date: _____

Overcoming the Fear of Failure

When a person tries something new, it is natural to fail at first. But that fear of failure can sometimes stop people from trying. If you accept the fact that you might fail the first time you do something, it can make trying easier. You will be free to learn from any mistakes. And you can make a plan about how you can do it differently next time. Messing up can be frustrating, but if you don't try, you won't ever succeed. Be brave and try again.

Directions: Finish the comic strip below. Show how the character overcomes failure.

Name: _____ Date: _____

Examining Biases

Imagine a man in a suit and tie with shiny shoes and a briefcase. The man next to him is wearing sweatpants and a T-shirt. If a person were asked which man was the owner of a big company, many people would choose the man in the suit. People sometimes make decisions based on assumptions instead of facts. This is called having a *bias*. It is natural to have biases, but try not to act on them. Since they are not based on facts, they can be wrong and hurt people's feelings.

Directions: Study the pictures, and answer the questions.

1. Which person might people assume is a gamer? Why?

_____

_____

2. Which person might people assume plays basketball? Why?

_____

_____

3. How do the questions show bias?

_____

_____

Focus on Community

Self-Awareness

Name: _____ Date: _____

Managing Your Emotions

There are so many things to do in a community. You might be in a big crowd at a concert or by yourself near a creek. These different situations can bring out many feelings. Taking a moment to think about your emotions is helpful. You can anticipate how you might feel. Then, you can react in a way that makes sense.

Directions: Read each situation. Write how you would feel in that situation and why.

1. On a cold winter day, your family heads to the outdoor ice rink to skate. The rink is packed with families. People everywhere are laughing, skating, and twirling around on the ice.

   _____

   _____

   _____

2. The baseball team from the local high school is playing in a championship game. You are sitting in the stands with friends. The game is almost over, and your team is winning.

   _____

   _____

   _____

3. After a long week at school, you are excited to take your book and read by the small pond in the park. As you sit down on a bench, a man begins mowing the grass around the pond.

   _____

   _____

   _____

Name: _____ Date: _____

Helping Others

Think about a time you helped someone else. It might have been a friend, teacher, or neighbor. If you want to be a helpful person, pay attention to people. You might give emotional help. This might mean inviting a lonely student to play. You might help them practically. This might mean opening the door for someone carrying heavy bags. Look for opportunities to help in your community. You will find them.

Directions: Draw ways to help each person in your community. Explain each drawing.

Focus on Community

Social Awareness

a friend who lost their ball at the park	a teacher carrying a large stack of papers
_____ _____	_____ _____
a person who dropped something at the store	a neighbor who lost their dog
_____ _____	_____ _____

Name: _____ Date: _____

Problem-Solving as a Team

Working with other people can be a lot of fun. You get to spend time together and work toward a common goal. But it is common for problems to come up. When this happens, you should talk about it, pinpoint the problem, and brainstorm solutions. Figure out the best way to keep going and complete the task. Learning how to work with others is a skill you will use your whole life.

Directions: Read the story, and answer the questions.

The Library Sign

Gabby's community was building a new library. She loved to read, so she couldn't wait for it to be finished. Gabby and her friends, Curtis and Aiko, were asked to help paint the sign for the children's wing. They met together to create a design and make a list of supplies they would need.

The first day they met to start work on the sign, Gabby was so excited. Aiko was a talented artist, so she was going to draw a child reading a book. Curtis brought letter stencils so they could make the words straight and neat. The library provided paint and brushes.

When they had everything set up, Aiko began sketching on the plain wooden sign. Curtis began laying out the stencils to spell the words. Gabby looked around. What was she supposed to do?

1. What problem does this group have?

_____

2. How can they solve this problem?

_____

_____

3. Describe a time you had to solve a problem when working with a group.

_____

_____

Name: _____ Date: _____

Using Critical-Thinking Skills

Many adults dream of owning their own businesses. Kids can own them, too. There are many ways young people can work to earn money. You could make and sell crafts. You could do chores for people in your community. If you follow through with your ideas, it might be a great way to make some money.

Directions: Answer the questions to help you plan a business.

1. List three different businesses you could start.

- _____
- _____
- _____

2. Which idea do you think is best?

_____

_____

3. What supplies will you need for your business?

_____   _____

_____   _____

_____   _____

4. Who will your customers be?

_____

_____

_____

5. How would your business make money?

_____

_____

_____

Focus on Community
Responsible Decision-Making

Name: _____ Date: _____

Focus on State

Self-Awareness

Connecting Feelings to Actions

Feelings can turn into actions. When you feel happy, you probably do different things than when you feel sad. Feelings can even cause things to happen within the government. Imagine someone learned about pollution in their state. It made them feel worried and upset. That feeling could lead them to take action. They might write letters to politicians. They might research solutions. They could lead a rally. Feelings that lead to action can make big changes.

Directions: Write two emotions you have had and why you felt that way. Explain what actions you might take because of those feelings. Then, draw one of those actions.

1. I felt _____ because _____.

I can _____

_____.

2. I felt _____ because _____.

I can _____

_____.

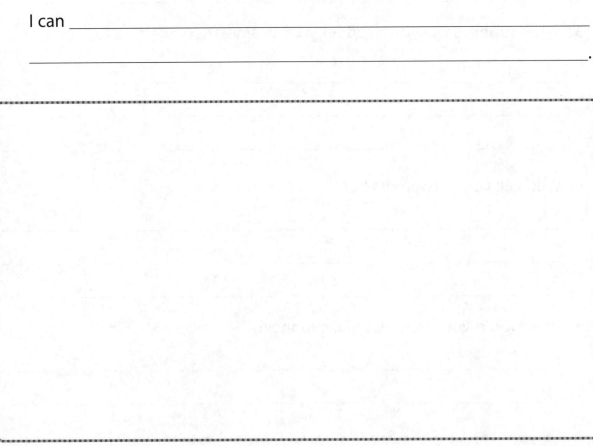

Name: _____ **Date:** _____

Setting Goals

Children, adults, schools, and governments can all set goals. The sizes and types of goals depend on who is making them. An individual might make a goal to eat healthy foods. A company's goal might be to increase sales. A state's goal might be to increase the use of solar energy. All these goals are important because they help people improve.

Directions: Write two goals you would like for your state. Draw each one.

Goal 1: _____

Goal 2: _____

Name: _____ Date: _____

Understanding Perspective

Being able to see things from a different perspective is a great skill to have. Imagine a state was going to make a new law about farming. They would have to look at it from different perspectives. What would farmers think? What would grocery store workers think? What would customers think? Each of those groups would see new laws a different way. Seeing different perspectives can help you make good choices.

Focus on State

Social Awareness

Directions: Read the story, and answer the questions.

Capitol Day

Fridays at the state capitol are open-office days. People come from all over the state to share their opinions with their elected leaders. DeShawn and Marc are both at the capitol today. They are meeting with their state senator.

"Schools need to require everyone to learn a foreign language!" Marc shared that he loves speaking Spanish and uses it in his everyday life. He is sure that other students would find it useful, too.

"I think everyone should take an extra science class," DeShawn countered. "Most of the jobs that will help our state involve science." His dad is an engineer, and DeShawn hopes to have a job like his dad's someday.

1. What is Marc's perspective? Why does he feel this way?

_____

_____

2. What is DeShawn's perspective? Why does he feel this way?

_____

_____

3. If you were the senator, what would you do? Why?

_____

_____

Name: _____ Date: _____

Leadership

Good leaders have many similar qualities. They should all follow through on what they say they will do. What a leader says matters. It is easy to make promises and talk about ideas. But if leaders want to gain the trust of people, they must do what they promise.

Directions: Read the story, and answer the questions.

The Candidate

Mr. Kent was running for office in his state. He wanted schools to have more access to technology. He gave speeches and talked about how much this would help students. People loved his idea, but they weren't sure it would happen.

Mr. Kent talked to school districts and listened to what they needed. He called a large technology company. He asked if they would be willing to donate supplies to schools. He had meetings with people in government. He shared his plan to use more of the state's budget to pay for technology in education.

On the day of the election, Mr. Kent felt nervous. Would the people vote for him?

1. What does Mr. Kent want to do for schools?

_____

_____

2. How does Mr. Kent try to make his ideas happen?

_____

_____

3. Would you vote for Mr. Kent? Why or why not?

_____

_____

Focus on State
Relationship Skills

Name: _____ Date: _____

Focus on State

Responsible Decision-Making

Reflecting on Decisions

People want to make good decisions. They might look at facts and data. They might think about the strengths and weaknesses of their choices. Then, they try to make the best decision they can. After the choice is made, it is a good idea to reflect. This means looking back and thinking about how things turned out. Reflecting can help a person, business, or government decide if their choice was a good one.

Directions: Think about a decision you made. Then, answer the questions to help you reflect on it.

1. What did you have to decide? What were your options?

   _____

   _____

   _____

   _____

2. How did you decide what to do?

   _____

   _____

3. What happened after you made your decision?

   _____

   _____

   _____

4. Do you think you made the right decision? Why or why not?

   _____

   _____

   _____

   _____

Name: _____ **Date:** _____

Honesty and Integrity

The internet is a big place. It has more information than can be imagined. People can read news, learn new information, and chat with others on social media. Because there is so much online, it is important to be honest. This means using facts for schoolwork in a responsible way. It also means being kind to others. Integrity is how you act when no one is looking. It's important to have integrity on the internet.

Directions: Read each situation, and answer the questions.

1. Liz is researching pandas for her essay. She finds some facts and copies them word-for-word into her essay. She thinks they will really impress her teacher.

   Did Liz do the right thing? Explain your answer.

   _____

   _____

   _____

2. Taisha has to draw a picture of the beach for art class, so she looks at pictures of beaches on the internet. She finds a few she likes and uses them as inspiration for her own drawing.

   Did Taisha do the right thing? Explain your answer.

   _____

   _____

   _____

3. Jon was playing an online game with a group of kids he did not know. He left a comment for one player saying they must be new because they weren't any good.

   Did Jon do the right thing? Explain your answer.

   _____

   _____

   _____

Focus on Self

Self-Awareness

Name: _____ Date: _____

Managing Screen Time

Screens are part of everyday life. People watch TV, work on computers, and play on tablets. All that screen time can be bad for your health. It can be a strain on vision, make it hard to sleep at night, and cause headaches. Not to mention, some kids might play on screens instead of playing outside. Using screens responsibly is important.

Directions: Read the tips for using screens in a healthy way. Then, answer the questions.

Tips for Safer Screen Time

1. Step away from screens for a few minutes every hour.

2. Set a timer to help limit screen time.

3. Dim the lights a bit when using a screen.

4. Consider using an app that limits blue light.

5. Stop using screens 30 minutes before bed.

1. Why is it important to limit screen time?

_____

_____

2. Which tip do you think you could start using? Why?

_____

_____

3. What tip would you add?

_____

_____

Name: _____ Date: _____

Understanding Different Rules

You are probably used to different rules at different places. You might need to raise your hand before speaking at school, but not at home. Running is fine in the park, but not in your kitchen. The internet has its own rules, too. Knowing and following those rules will help keep you safe when you are online.

Directions: Circle whether each rule is a good safety rule for using the internet.

1. Choose strong passwords.   yes   no

2. Use the internet for as long as you need.   yes   no

3. Share your personal information with anyone who asks.   yes   no

4. Limit the time you spend online.   yes   no

5. Use the same password on different sites.   yes   no

6. Ask an adult before downloading something.   yes   no

7. Tell an adult if something online makes you uncomfortable.   yes   no

8. Post pictures of yourself online.   yes   no

Name: _____ Date: _____

Focus on Self

Relationship Skills

Resisting Peer Pressure

When your friends try to talk you into doing something, it is called *peer pressure*. They might pressure you to do something good, such as practicing your math facts. But often, friends might pressure you to do something you know you shouldn't. It can be hard to stand up to that type of pressure. But doing the right thing is always better.

Directions: Read the story, and answer the questions.

The App

"You've got to check out this new app," Leo said to Jackson after school. "It connects you to other people who play the same sports as you."

Jackson watched as Leo went through the app. It did look really cool, and Jackson loved soccer and swimming. It could be a lot of fun.

"Go ahead and download it," Leo said.

"Well, I'm not really supposed to get new apps unless my mom says it's okay," Jackson admitted.

"There nothing bad about this app, and your mom won't even know," Leo argued.

1. Describe the peer pressure in the story.

_____

_____

_____

2. What would you do if you were Jackson?

_____

_____

_____

3. What could you do if your friends are pressuring you?

_____

_____

Name: _____ **Date:** _____

Making Good Decisions

The internet is a great place to do research. There are millions of websites available with the touch of a key. But not all sites are trustworthy. When you do research, you have to decide which sites to get information from. You don't want to use pages that were written a long time ago. They might have outdated information. You also do not want to use pages that have a strong opinion either. Sites that end in .gov or .edu are usually good. And it's a good sign if sites show where they got their information. Using trustworthy sites will help you learn the right information.

Directions: Create a poster to teach others about finding trustworthy websites. Use information on this page, and add your own ideas.

Name: _____ Date: _____

Focus on Neighborhood

Self-Awareness

Identifying Your Emotions

When people react to events, it can involve their whole bodies. If something good or bad or scary happens, you feel emotions. But often, your body also responds. Maybe your heart beats fast, or your face has a huge smile. Physical things can affect the way your body feels, too. You might feel cold, sweaty, or tired depending on the event. Paying attention to the way your body feels is important.

Directions: Read each situation that might happen in your neighborhood. Write the emotion you would feel and how your body would respond.

1. You find out your neighbor is very sick and has to go to the hospital.

   _____

   _____

2. You are playing in the pool on a summer day with other kids on your street.

   _____

   _____

3. Your family wins your neighborhood's "Most Beautiful Yard" contest.

   _____

   _____

4. You shovel the driveways for several neighbors on a snowy day.

   _____

   _____

Name: _____ Date: _____

Using I-Messages

When you talk with others, it is good to use I-messages. This means you begin sentences explaining how you feel, instead of what the other person has said or done. This can be helpful during conflicts. For example, suppose someone is often late. You could say, "I am frustrated when I have to wait for you." Or, "I like it when you are on time." Saying "You are always late," can make the other person feel defensive.

Directions: Read the short play, and answer the questions.

The Tree Branch

Two men live next door to each other. The branches of a large tree in one yard hang into the other yard.

Mr. Valdez: Your tree's branches are out of control! Can't you do something about it?

Mr. McPhee: I feel like tree branches are natural and normal. But I am sorry they make you upset.

Mr. Valdez: You should at least come rake up all of the leaves your tree is dropping in my yard.

Mr. McPhee: I understand it's inconvenient, but we all have yardwork. I talked to an expert, and the branches are not overgrown. I would really appreciate it if you would rake your yard.

1. Which man is using I-messages? _____

2. How would you describe Mr. Valdez? How does his language show his character?

   _____

   _____

3. How would you describe Mr. McPhee? How does his language show his character?

   _____

   _____

Name: _____ Date: _____

Recognizing Others' Strengths

A neighborhood is full of many different types of people. They might be quiet or outgoing. Some might be good at organizing events. Other people might be very thoughtful. There might even be hosts who throw neighborhood parties. The people in your life have different talents and strengths. They would love to know that you appreciate them.

Directions: Draw someone in your neighborhood you know and admire. Fill in the thought bubbles with words and phrases that describe their strengths.

Name: _____ **Date:** _____

Communicating Effectively

When people have a conversation, they take turns being the sender and the receiver. When you are the receiver, there are things you can do to give feedback. Your facial expressions show you are listening. You might smile, laugh, or frown. Your body language can also be feedback. You might nod, sit up straight, or touch the sender. Your feedback shows whether you understand what the sender is saying.

Directions: Complete the table to describe the feedback you would give for each message.

	Facial Expression	Body Language	What You Would Say
"My dog got really sick and died yesterday."			
"My grandparents are coming tomorrow. I haven't seen them in a year!"			
"I lost my wallet a few days ago and can't find it anywhere."			
"I jumped out at my brother, and he was so startled he dropped his plate of food."			

Focus on Neighborhood

Relationship Skills

Name: _____ Date: _____

Identifying Big and Small Problems

In life, there are big problems and small problems. If a problem is small, you can solve it on your own. You won't need to involve others. For big problems, you will need help from an adult. A family member, neighbor, or friend could help you. Understanding the difference between big and small problems is helpful. Solving small problems on your own will help you be independent. Asking for help will give you support and help you prepare for the future.

Directions: Draw and describe a big and a small problem in your neighborhood. The problems can be from your real life or your imagination.

Big Problem

_____

_____

_____

_____

Small Problem

_____

_____

_____

_____

Focus on Neighborhood
Responsible Decision-Making

Name: _____ Date: _____

Focus on Friends

Self-Awareness

Growth Mindset

When people have a growth mindset, they think they can learn about and improve in any area. When people have a fixed mindset, they think they can't change their abilities. This can stop them from trying new things or from working hard to get better at a skill or talent. The good news is, people can learn to have a growth mindset. Changing a mindset can provide new opportunities.

Directions: Imagine a friend said each fixed mindset statement. Write what you would say to help them change their mindset.

1. "I'm so bad at spelling. I always get questions wrong on spelling tests. I guess I'll always be a bad speller."

   _____

   _____

   _____

2. "I played on a soccer team when I was little. I didn't like running around and always kicked the ball sideways instead of straight. Soccer just isn't my sport."

   _____

   _____

   _____

3. "I studied for that test and still got a bad grade. I should just stop studying for tests. What's the point?"

   _____

   _____

   _____

Name: _____ Date: _____

Managing Your Emotions

Sometimes, people react with big feelings. They might be sad, happy, or angry. But they are feeling them very intensely. When emotions get very big, there can be problems. It can be hard to talk to a person who feels this way, and they might get out of control. When you are feeling big emotions, it is important to try to de-escalate. This means to reduce something and make it not as strong. Deep breathing and taking a mental break can help. So can talking with someone or doing a minute of physical activity.

Directions: Read the story, and answer the questions.

Dance Routine

Jayla saw a new dance routine and couldn't wait to show it to her friend, Kylie. That afternoon, they watched the video of the dance over and over. Soon, Jayla was doing it on her own.

Kylie was struggling. She kept forgetting the steps.

"This is impossible!" she groaned, and flopped down on the couch. "I'm never going to figure this out." She kicked a magazine on the floor.

"Sure you will," Jayla said encouragingly.

"No! I don't even want to do this stupid dance!" Kylie yelled.

1. Do you think Kylie needs to de-escalate her emotions? Why or why not?

_____

2. What do you think Jayla should do?

_____

_____

3. How would you advise Kylie to calm down?

_____

_____

Name: _____ Date: _____

> ## Noticing Needs
>
> Most friends would probably call themselves helpful. They are happy to lend a pencil or share a piece of candy. But there might be times when friends need help, and no one notices. Paying attention to the needs of others can help you be even more helpful.

Directions: Answer the questions to find a way to help a friend.

1. Observe your friends. What do you notice?

_____

_____

2. Which friend can you help? What can you do?

_____

_____

3. What is your plan to help? Write at least three steps.

_____

_____

_____

4. How does it feel to help friends?

_____

_____

_____

_____

_____

Name: _____ Date: _____

Receiving and Decoding Messages

People can communicate with verbal messages. But messages can also be sent with gestures and body language. Facial expressions show meaning, too.

Focus on Friends

Relationship skills

Directions: Draw two people having an argument. Include body language and facial expressions that show their feelings. Write what they are saying in the speech bubbles.

© Shell Education

Name: _____ **Date:** _____

Overcoming the Fear of Failure

Trying new things always comes with a risk. But even though you might fail, that isn't necessarily a bad thing. In fact, trying again and overcoming failure can be great. It teaches you how to keep going and how to figure out new ways to try something. And the sense of accomplishment when you succeed is amazing.

Directions: Read the prompt. Then, create a comic strip to show what will happen before, during, and after.

Learning a New Trick

Two friends just got new skateboards and want to learn a trick called an ollie. An ollie is when a person jumps over an object and the skateboard seems to be stuck to their feet. They have never skateboarded before. They both think they will fail the first time they try the trick. Show the two friends before, during, and after they learn to do an ollie.

Before

During

After

Name: _____ Date: _____

Developing Interests

People have all sort of hobbies, interests, and talents. They may use them in their jobs or for their own enjoyment. They can also use their interests to help others. If someone knows how to build things, they could help make tables and benches for parks. Or maybe someone is a good singer. They could sing the national anthem before an event. Communities depend on the talents of their people.

Directions: Complete the chart by writing things you are good at and how they could help your community. Then, draw one idea from your chart.

Interest, Talent, or Hobby	How It Can Help Your Community

Name: _____ Date: _____

Using Self-Talk

Even people who are hard workers can have days when they don't feel motivated. But the work still has to be done. So those people use self-discipline. They may also use self-talk to motivate themselves. You might also be faced with something you don't want to do. It could be homework, chores, or guitar practice. Try self-talk. You might tell yourself the reason you need to do it or give yourself encouragement to finish. You could even offer yourself a small reward.

Directions: Write how you would use self-talk to complete each task.

1. Your community park is filled with trash. So your family volunteers to help pick it up. You know it will be better when it's done, but this job sounds so boring.

   _____

   _____

2. You have band practice tonight. You'd rather just hang out at home and watch TV with your family.

   _____

   _____

3. It is raining outside, but your neighbor's dog really needs a walk. They're on vacation and asked you to take care of her. You don't want to get cold and wet.

   _____

   _____

4. Your teacher gave math and science homework today. You'd rather play your video game, but your family rule is to do homework first.

   _____

   _____

Name: _____ Date: _____

Focus on Community

Social Awareness

Accepting Gratitude

You probably do kind things every day. You might give compliments or do a favor for someone. You might help others or simply be a good friend. When people are shown kindness, they often show gratitude with words or actions. There are many ways for you to accept their gratitude.

Directions: Read the text, and answer the questions.

What to Say?

People say a lot of different things when the other person says, "Thank you." They might say, "No problem," or "No big deal." Some people think these responses don't really accept gratitude. They feel like it shows what the helper did was not important. They think "You're welcome" is the only right way to answer. Other people think those responses are fine to use. They are common, casual, and their meaning is understood.

1. Do you think saying "no problem" is a good way to accept thanks? Why or why not?

_____

_____

_____

2. What do you usually say when you accept thanks? Why?

_____

_____

_____

3. Why is it important to respond when someone thanks you?

_____

_____

_____

Name: _____ Date: _____

Offering Help

There are always things happening in a community. People are busy working, playing, and living their lives. In the midst of all that, people sometimes need help. When bad things happen, people in a community can help. Time, supplies, money, and support can mean a lot to people who need them.

Directions: Read the story, and answer the questions.

The House Fire

Tess stood on the sidewalk, staring at the Jacksons' house. The fire had raged the night before, but it was out now. Everyone was safe, but the house would need a lot of repairs.

All around her, neighbors were doing what they could to help. Tess's mom was collecting clothes from local thrift stores. Her dad organized a group to begin to fix the damage. Others were making food, offering the Jacksons a place to stay, and taking care of the children.

Tess wanted to help, too. She heard Mrs. Jackson mention that all of their photo albums had been lost in the fire. Tess sent an email to everyone she could think of and asked them to email her any pictures they had of the Jacksons. She planned to print them and make a new album for the family.

1. How do the neighbors offer their support? _____

_____

2. Why does Tess decide to email neighbors? _____

_____

3. How do you think the Jackson family will respond to the new photo album?

_____

_____

_____

Name: _____ Date: _____

Focus on Community

Responsible Decision-Making

Solving Problems

Some problems are unavoidable. People will disagree, things won't work out, plans will change, or items will break. That's why being able to solve problems is so important. Solutions can be split into two types. One is constructive. This means the solution involves making things better. It leaves people feeling satisfied. The other type is destructive. This means the solution might fix the problem, but it does not make anyone happy.

Directions: Read the story, and answer the questions.

Softball Team

The community softball league was very popular. Many adults enjoyed playing. This year, the city made a new rule that players had to be younger than 60. City leaders felt that it might be unsafe for older players to be in the league. This upset many players. It didn't seem fair, and they talked to the city council. The council came up with two solutions. One was to stop the league. The other was to require a doctor's note for players to join.

1. Which solution is constructive? Explain your answer.

_____

_____

_____

2. Which solution is destructive? Explain your answer.

_____

_____

_____

3. Write your own constructive solution to this problem.

_____

_____

_____

Name: _____ **Date:** _____

Social Identity

Nicknames have a lot of meanings. Sometimes, they are a shortened version of a full name. Other times, they tell a little about the person or thing. Many states have nicknames. California is the Golden State. Rhode Island is the Ocean State. Minnesota is the Land of 10,000 Lakes. Each state nickname shares something about the state. It might be about its history, location, or resources.

Directions: Answer the questions.

1. What is your nickname? If you don't have one, make one up for yourself.

   _____

2. Do you like your nickname? Why or why not? What does it mean?

   _____

   _____

   _____

3. What are some nicknames you have for family or friends? Why do you call them that?

   _____

   _____

4. If you could choose a new nickname for your state, what would it be? Explain your answer.

   _____

   _____

Name: Candy

Name: Rick

Name: Chuy

Name: Rose

Focus on State
Self-Awareness

Name: _____ Date: _____

Focus on State

Self-Management

Setting Goals

Individuals, businesses, and governments can all make goals. Some goals are too big to do at once. It's a good idea to break those into smaller goals. Then, give each goal a time limit. A state may have a goal to use more solar energy. The one-year goal could be to install solar panels on courthouses. The five-year goal could be to install them on all state agency buildings. The ten-year goal could be to install them on all government buildings. Splitting up the big goal makes it easier to achieve.

Directions: Think of a big goal you would like to accomplish. Then, answer the questions.

1. What is your big goal?

   _____

2. Divide your goal into two smaller goals.

   • _____

   • _____

3. How much time will you take to finish the first goal?

   _____

4. How much time will you take to finish the second goal?

   _____

5. Draw yourself achieving your goal.

Name: _____ Date: _____

Identifying Different Rules

Laws can be made by a state or city. Laws about crimes, property, and speed limits are made by states. Laws about rent, safety, and how certain land will be used are made by cities. State laws must be followed in each city. This can happen in schools, too. A school might have certain rules, but teachers might make specific rules for their classrooms. The school rules must be followed in the entire school, but the classroom rules are for that room only.

Directions: List three rules a school might have and three different rules a classroom might have. Then, answer the questions.

School Rules	Classroom Rules

1. Why would a classroom need different rules from the school?

   _____

   _____

2. Why might one city or state have different laws from another?

   _____

   _____

Name: _____ Date: _____

Focus on State

Relationship Skills

Appreciating Different Cultures

Many cultures are present in each state. Some of the people might have come from all over the world. They may have unique traditions. They might follow a certain religion or speak a different language. The people are a vital part of where they live.

Directions: Flags are made to represent countries, states, and groups of people. Draw a flag that represents different cultures in your state. Then, explain your flag.

_____

_____

_____

_____

Name: _____ Date: _____

Making Good Decisions

State governments have to make big decisions, from where to put a bridge to how to spend millions or billions of dollars. They have to choose how to spend money or where to build a new bridge. The leaders have to be wise when making these decisions. They might compare the pros (good things) against the cons (bad things). You can do this when you make decisions, too. Weighing pros and cons will help you choose wisely.

Directions: Think of a decision you could make. It could be from real life or your imagination. Create a list of pros and cons. Then, answer the question.

Decision to Make: _____

Pros	Cons

1. What did you decide? Why?

_____

_____

Name: _____ Date: _____

Focus on Self
Self-Awareness

Naming Your Emotions

Taking a moment to think about how you feel is smart. It helps you understand your behavior and responses. There are many ways you can name your emotions. You could think to yourself or talk about it with someone. You could also write about it in a journal. Some people even express their feelings through poetry.

Directions: Haiku is a type of three-line poem. The first and third lines have five syllables, and the second line has seven. The lines do not rhyme and do not have to be complete sentences. Read the example haiku about an emotion. Then, write your own.

Courage

my heart is racing

the audience is waiting

take a breath and start

Title: _____

_____
(5 syllables)

_____
(7 syllables)

_____
(5 syllables)

Name: _____ Date: _____

Setting Goals

You likely have many goals. Having goals can help keep you focused, and you can set them for all different parts of your life. Knowing where you need goals in your life is an important skill.

Directions: Write a goal for each area of your life.

Family

Learning

Friends

Sport or Hobby

Name: _____ Date: _____

Helping Others

Some people are described as helpful. Maybe someone has even called you helpful. But what does it mean to be helpful? A helpful person looks for opportunities. They notice other people. If they see a need or a problem, they think about what they could do, and then they do it.

Directions: Answer the questions.

1. Who is a helpful person you know? What makes them helpful?

_____

_____

2. Do you think you are a helpful person? Why or why not?

_____

_____

3. How could you be even more helpful?

_____

_____

4. Draw yourself helping someone.

Name: _____ Date: _____

Avoiding Communication Blockers

When people talk, they want their messages to be understood. There are many things they can do to help this happen. But there are also things they should avoid. These communication blockers can stop a message from getting to the listener. They can also be rude and hurtful. Here are some examples.

insulting—being disrespectful or rude

judging—deciding whether something is good, bad, or has value

sarcasm—saying the opposite of what you mean in an insulting, mocking way

threatening—making someone do something by saying something bad will happen if they don't

Directions: Write which communication blocker each person is using.

1. "If you don't let me borrow that, I won't be your friend anymore."

_____

2. "You didn't get the math problem correct? Wow, you're super smart."

_____

3. "There is no way your idea is going to work."

_____

4. "Your shirt is really ugly."

_____

Name: _____ Date: _____

Focus on Self

Responsible Decision-Making

Apologizing

No matter how hard people try, they will make mistakes. When this happens, they need to apologize. That means more than just saying, "I'm sorry." That's a good start, though. A true apology also shares what someone did wrong. It states how the person will change their behavior. Giving or receiving a sincere apology will help fix a problem.

Directions: Write a true apology for each situation. Be sure to include all the steps.

Step 1: Say, "I'm sorry."

Step 2: State what you did wrong.

Step 3: Explain how you will change your behavior.

1. Your parent has told you not to play ball in the house. You kicked a soccer ball inside anyway. It knocked over a glass, and it broke.

_____

_____

_____

_____

2. Your friend needs a book for school, and you promised she could borrow your copy. You forgot to bring it.

_____

_____

_____

_____

Name: _____   Date: _____

Advocating for Yourself

It can be hard for people to stand up for themselves. They might be afraid to speak up or nervous they will make someone upset. They might even wonder if they are right to speak up in the first place. But advocating for yourself is good. If there is something wrong or something you want to change, you need to let people know. You can be calm and polite and still share your thoughts.

Directions: Write one thing you could advocate for in your home. Then, answer the questions.

1. What will you speak up about?

_____

_____

2. Who will you talk to about it?

_____

3. Why do you want this change?

_____

_____

_____

4. Why do you think it should happen?

_____

_____

_____

Name: _____ Date: _____

Focus on Family

Self-Management

Using Calendars

A lot of activities can happen in a month. That's why many families use a calendar. They can write the events for the month. This helps keep a family organized.

Directions: Look at the family's calendar. Then, answer the questions.

Sunday	Monday	Tuesday	Wednesday	Thursday	Friday	Saturday
1	2 7:00 p.m. Sonja: violin lesson	3	4 12:00 p.m. Dad: lunch with Grandpa	5	6	7
8	9 7:00 p.m. Sonja: violin lesson	10	11	12 10:00 a.m. Mom: doctor	13	14 9:30 a.m. Ty: hockey game
15 3:00 p.m. Ty: hockey game	16 7:00 p.m. Sonja: violin lesson	17	18 12:00 p.m. Dad: lunch with Grandpa	19	20	21
22	23 7:00 p.m. Sonja: violin lesson	24 8:00 a.m. Mom: conference call	25	26 4:30 p.m. Dad: haircut	27 5:00 p.m. Ty: hockey game	28

1. Which events happen more than once? _____

2. When does Mom have a conference call? _____

3. When is Ty's last hockey game of the month? _____

4. On the calendar, add a family game night at 7:00 p.m. to the first Saturday of the month.

Name: _____ Date: _____

Taking Others' Perspectives

If you pay attention to the people in your family, you can learn about them. Look for clues in what they talk about, how they act, their body language, and facial expressions. When you notice these things, it can help you figure out how they are feeling. This can make you more sensitive to their moods.

Directions: Read the situations, and write how each family member might be feeling and how you know.

1. Jesse's dad is trying to put together a new bookshelf. He has the parts on the floor and is holding the instructions. He looks from the parts to the paper over and over, rubbing his forehead.

   _____

   _____

   _____

   _____

2. Diane's mom just got home from work. She drops her coat and bag on the chair instead of hanging them up. Then, she flops on the couch, leans her head back, and closes her eyes.

   _____

   _____

   _____

   _____

3. Martin's older sister is watching a movie. She is slowly shaking her head. He notices a box of tissues beside her and that she keeps wiping her eyes.

   _____

   _____

   _____

   _____

Focus on Family

Social Awareness

Name: _____ Date: _____

Focus on Family

Relationship skills

Nonverbal Communication

People often depend on words to get their meanings across. But gestures and nonverbal communication can share meaning, too. Even if you were in a situation where you couldn't talk, you could still nod or shake your head. You could use your hands and make gestures. It might be challenging, but it would still get the job done. It could even be fun, like playing a game of charades.

Directions: Read the sentences. Explain how you could communicate them to your family without saying any words. Describe the facial expressions or gestures you would use.

1. Do you want to go swimming?

_____

_____

2. It is time to eat lunch.

_____

_____

3. It is cold outside.

_____

_____

4. I love baseball.

_____

_____

Directions: Think of your own sentence, and see if a classmate or family member can guess what you're saying. Write what happens.

_____

_____

_____

Name: _____ **Date:** _____

How Behavior Affects Others

Your actions affect others. They can especially affect your family because you spend so much time with them. This can be a positive thing. Your good mood might rub off on others. But it can also be a negative thing. Being impatient or angry can make others feel the same way. You can't always help how you feel. But you can think about how your mood and behavior affect other members of your family.

Directions: Read each situation. Draw a picture to show how the actions might affect a family member.

1. August yelled at his little sister after she accidentally lost his lucky rock.

2. During dinner, Sally told her grandma how much she loves her cooking.

Name: _____ Date: _____

Examining Prejudices

Prejudice is an unfair feeling about a person or group of people. It might be based on skin color. But it can also be based on gender or religion. People should think about any unfair feelings they may have about others. You can speak out against prejudice. You can stand up for yourself if it happens to you. People can make a change by working together. All people should treat others as equals.

Directions: Read the story, and answer the questions.

The Robotics Team

Sonja was new at school, but she already loved it. Her math teacher asked her to join the school's robotics team. She walked into the gym after school for her first meeting. She noticed she was the only girl, but she didn't mind. A few of the boys smiled at her, but one named Peter was frowning.

"I'm Sonja," she said to the group. "I'm new here, and am joining the team."

"Do you even know anything about robots?" Peter asked. "Or electronics at all? I'm pretty sure girls are terrible at this stuff."

"Peter, leave her alone," another boy said. "You don't know anything about her."

1. What example of prejudice do you see in the story?

_____

_____

2. How does the second boy stand up to prejudice?

_____

_____

3. What types of prejudice have you noticed in real life?

_____

_____

Focus on School

Self-Awareness

Name: _____ **Date:** _____

Managing Your Emotions

School can be stressful sometimes. You might get angry with a classmate or get frustrated if an assignment is hard. If you are feeling upset or stressed, it is good to have a few ways to deescalate. Recall that de-escalate means to bring your emotions back to a calm level. Deep breathing can help. So can stepping away and getting some personal space. Exercising can decrease your stress, too.

Directions: Read the steps that can help you de-escalate. Follow the steps. Then, answer the questions.

> **Step 1:** If possible, find some personal space.
>
> **Step 2:** Take deep breaths.
>
> **Step 3:** Wiggle your toes and fingers.
>
> **Step 4:** Count to 10.
>
> Repeat all the steps until you feel calm.

1. How did you feel after following the steps?

_____

_____

_____

_____

2. Describe a time when this exercise could help you decrease your stress.

_____

_____

_____

_____

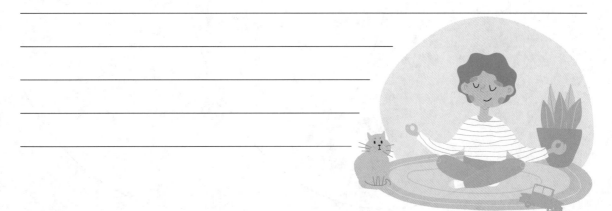

Name: _____ Date: _____

Understanding Different Rules

Different places have different rules. Even the same types of places, such as homes, schools, or businesses, don't all have the same rules. Individual places make rules based on what makes sense for the people who live, learn, or work there. Big schools and small schools might have different rules. So might private and public schools. Schools that meet online may be different from those that meet in person.

Directions: Imagine a school is starting an outdoor classroom. It will need different rules than an indoor one. Create a Venn diagram that shows at least two rules for each learning space.

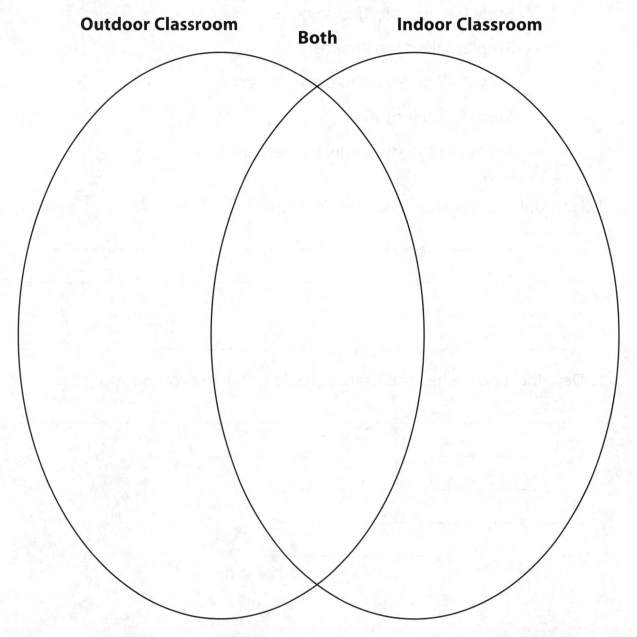

Focus on School
Social Awareness

Name: _____ Date: _____

Understanding Cultures

Students learn in schools all over the world. The schools might be big brick buildings or small wooden ones. They might be in church basements or the great outdoors. But all students learn and prepare for their futures. Learning about schools in other countries and cultures can be interesting and fun.

Directions: Read the text, and answer the questions.

School in Brazil

Brazil is a large country in South America. Most of the people there speak Portuguese. Schools are split into primary and secondary. Only about 60 percent of students attend secondary school. Many need to work and earn money to help their families. The school day lasts about five hours. Their school year starts in February and ends in November. Schools do not have sports teams or music classes. But students can play on community teams and take lessons. Students in Brazil might play soccer, volleyball, and basketball.

1. How is your school like school in Brazil? How is it different?

_____

_____

_____

_____

2. What would you like most about going to school in Brazil? Why?

_____

_____

3. What would you not like about going to school in Brazil? Why?

_____

_____

Focus on School

Relationship Skills

Name: _____ Date: _____

Focus on School

Responsible Decision-Making

Big and Small Reactions

When people learn new information, they have reactions. Depending on the news, they might be big or small. Amazing news might be met with a big reaction of cheering. But for unexciting news, a person might just smile or nod. Reactions can also depend on personality. Two people can hear the same news but have different reactions.

Directions: Draw a person having a big reaction in the first comic. Draw a person having a small reaction in the second comic.

Name: _____ **Date:** _____

Contributing to Your Community

There are so many ways people can help their communities. They can donate money or supplies. They can volunteer or lead a group. They can serve others or think of brand-new ideas. It can be hard to know where to start if you want to help. One thing you can do is think about the different seasons. Your community has needs in the summer, and they are probably different from needs in the winter. Focusing on the holidays, weather, and events in a season can give your ideas a boost.

Directions: Draw one way you can help your community in each season.

Spring	Fall

Summer	Winter

Focus on Community

Self-Awareness

Name: _____ **Date:** _____

Managing Your Emotions

When people hear bad news, they might have different reactions. Some people might be mad, some might be scared, and others might be worried. All of these emotions are normal. Knowing what to do with those feelings is important. You can use different strategies to help manage your feelings when you hear bad news.

Directions: Read the story, and answer the questions.

Factory Closing

Jemma could tell her parents were worried. The big factory in town announced it was closing in just a few weeks, and both of Jemma's parents worked there. A lot of her neighbors worked there, too. What would happen to their community if all those people lost their jobs? Jemma felt angry and scared that the factory was closing.

While her parents talked, Jemma went for a bike ride around her block. The sun felt good on her back, and the wind was cool on her cheeks. When she came back to the house, she put on some music and grabbed her journal. She wrote about what had happened, how she felt, and added a few questions she had.

Later at dinner, she took a deep breath and said, "I heard about the factory closing. Is it okay if I ask you a few questions?"

"Of course," her dad said. "You can always ask us anything."

1. Why is Jemma upset?

_____

2. How does Jemma manage her feelings?

_____

3. Which strategy do you think would work best for you? Why?

_____

_____

Name: _____ Date: _____

Recognizing Others' Strengths

A community is made of many types of people. They work together to help things run smoothly and safely. There are many types of jobs, and they are all important. It takes different skills and strengths to do different jobs well. Recognizing what others are good at is a nice way to show that you appreciate them.

Directions: Study the list of jobs in a community. Write one strength, skill, or talent a person would need to have that job. Then, write a story involving at least two of those helpers working together in your community.

1. nurse _____

2. teacher _____

3. business owner _____

4. chef _____

5. police officer _____

6. artist _____

7. librarian _____

_____

_____

_____

_____

_____

_____

_____

_____

_____

Name: _____   Date: _____

Problem-Solving as a Team

Problems are common, and solving them on your own can be hard. It is nice to have others around for support. There are more people to come up with solutions. You can all share the work to solve the problem.

Directions: Read the problem, and brainstorm two different solutions. Then, choose one, and explain why you think it is best.

Trivia Night

A group of people in your community are planning a trivia night fundraiser. The money will help start a new after-school program for students. The event is going to be held in a local restaurant. A week before the big night, a pipe bursts in the kitchen. The restaurant can no longer host trivia night. How can the group solve this problem?

1. Solution 1: _____

_____

2. Solution 2: _____

_____

3. Which solution do you choose? Why?

_____

_____

_____

Focus on Community

Relationship Skills

Name: _____ Date: _____

Reflecting on Community

Each community is unique and special in its own way. Think about where you live. What do you like about it? What do you wish was different? Reflecting about your community is a good way to appreciate it and think about how you could help make it even better.

Directions: Draw your ideal community. Include at least four details, and explain each one.

Focus on Community

Responsible Decision-Making

_____

_____

_____

_____

Name: _____ Date: _____

Honesty

People are faced with choices about honesty every day. Should they tell the truth? Or should they try to hide or lie about it? This also happens to government leaders. Their honesty can affect others much more. It can be hard to tell the truth sometimes, but being dishonest has consequences.

Directions: Read the story, and answer the questions.

The Animal Shelter

When Marco was elected governor of his state, he made people a promise. He said he would use a small portion of taxes to fund animal shelters around the state. He had been in office for a while, but no money was going to the shelters. A group of animal lovers were beginning to ask questions.

The truth was, Marco had made a mistake. There was less money than he thought, and there was not enough to fund the animal shelters. He wasn't sure what to do. If he told the people the truth, they would not trust him anymore. They might not vote for some new laws he wanted to make. They might not even elect him again!

1. What is Marco's problem?

_____

2. If you were Marco, how would you feel about the problem?

_____

3. What advice would you give Marco?

_____

_____

4. Write about a time you were honest. How did it feel?

_____

_____

_____

Name: _____ Date: _____

Trying New Things

There are many benefits to experiencing new places. It can be exciting and interesting. New places can help you meet new people and let you try new things. Your state likely has many places you have never seen. Visiting a new place takes a little planning, but it is worth it.

Directions: Answer the questions to make a plan to visit a new place in your state. You may need to do some internet research to learn about places in your state you can visit.

1. What new place would you like to visit? Why?

_____

2. What supplies will you need?

_____

_____

3. What preparation will this visit require? Who will help you?

_____

_____

4. What might you learn or appreciate at this place? How will it help you?

_____

_____

5. Draw yourself visiting the new place. Be sure to include the people who will visit with you.

Focus on State

Self-Management

Name: _____ Date: _____

Understanding Others' Emotions

People sometimes share their emotions with words. That makes them easy to understand. But not everyone likes to be so open about their feelings. You can still figure it out though. People's actions and behaviors can show how they feel. Connecting how people act to how they feel helps you see their perspectives.

Directions: Read the text, and answer the question.

Two Speakers

Two people are trying to be elected as a state official. They are giving speeches. The first person speaks quietly into the microphone. He often looks down at his notes. He stumbles over his words as he speaks. The second person speaks loudly into the microphone. She looks at the crowd. She uses facial expressions and gestures as she speaks.

1. What do the actions of the two people tell you about their feelings?

_____

_____

Directions: Draw a person who is angry and a person who is happy. Be sure their actions show how they are feeling.

Name: _____ **Date:** _____

Communication Helpers

You will give many presentations in your life. Maybe you already have. State officials and people in business give presentations all the time. Visual aids can help. They can be posters, whiteboards, or computer screens. Aids might have pictures, graphs, or video clips. Good visual aids can make a speech more interesting. They also make it easier to understand.

Directions: Create a visual aid to help explain something you are learning in school.

Name: _____ Date: _____

Focus on State

Responsible Decision-Making

Anticipating Consequences

Actions have consequences. Sometimes they are good, and sometimes they are not. It is possible for a person's actions to only affect themself. But often, the actions of one person impact others. This is why it is smart for people to think about what they do. Their actions could help or hurt others.

Directions: Read the story, and answer the questions.

The Field Trip

Nora's class was visiting the art museum for a field trip. In the morning, her class stayed together for a tour. In the afternoon, they split into groups with parent volunteers. Nora liked the sculptures and wanted to go back for another look.

As the group made their way back to the sculpture room, two of the students in her group began acting out. They used loud voices and said rude things about the artwork they passed. They tried to play tag around the displays. One of them even reached out to touch a piece of art.

"This behavior is not acceptable," the parent volunteer said. "We will all need to go wait in the front lobby until the other groups are finished looking."

Nora was so disappointed. She wouldn't get her second visit to the sculptures after all.

1. How do the students' behavior affect Nora? _____

_____

2. Do you think the situation is fair? Why or why not? _____

_____

3. Share a time when you experienced a consequence (either good or bad) because of someone else's behavior.

_____

_____

Name: _____ Date: _____

Growth Mindset

Recall that there are two ways to approach a new skill. One is a growth mindset, which means you think you can get better at a skill with hard work and practice. The other is a fixed mindset, which means you believe you are born with certain skills, and practice will not make you better. You might be good at singing, playing a sport, solving math problems, or writing stories. Those skills might come easily to you. But practice and hard work will still lead to growth and improvement.

Directions: Answer the questions.

1. Write three things you have a natural ability to do or that come easily to you.

   • _____

   • _____

   • _____

2. What can you do to become even better at these things?

   • _____

   • _____

   • _____

3. Write one thing that is a little hard for you to do.

   _____

4. What can you do to improve at that thing?

   _____

   _____

   _____

   _____

Name: _____ Date: _____

Focus on Self

Self-Management

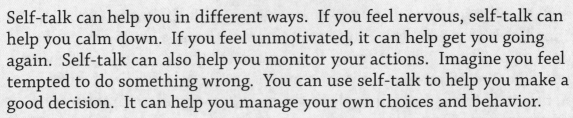

Using Self-Talk

Self-talk can help you in different ways. If you feel nervous, self-talk can help you calm down. If you feel unmotivated, it can help get you going again. Self-talk can also help you monitor your actions. Imagine you feel tempted to do something wrong. You can use self-talk to help you make a good decision. It can help you manage your own choices and behavior.

Directions: Write what you could say to yourself in each situation to help manage your choices and behavior. Then, answer the question.

1. You overhear two students talking about a classmate. They are not saying kind things. You think about joining in their conversation. You want to tell them about a time the classmate bothered you.

   _____

   _____

2. Your parent tells you it's time to go to sleep, but you want to keep reading. You think about getting the flashlight out from under your bed and reading another chapter.

   _____

   _____

3. You have to watch a video clip for science homework. You don't have to turn anything in for it. You think about not watching the video.

   _____

   _____

4. How else could you use self-talk in your life to help monitor your behavior? Be specific.

   _____

   _____

   _____

   _____

Name: _____ Date: _____

Recognizing Others' Strengths

Sometimes, it is easy to notice other people's strengths. You might want to be more like those other people. But what if you could also focus on your strengths? Focus on what you like about a certain person, and then look for those traits in yourself. You will probably find a lot of the same things.

Focus on Self

Social Awareness

Directions: Answer the questions about a character in a book you admire.

1. Draw the character.

2. Why do you admire this character?

_____

_____

_____

3. What do you have in common with this character?

_____

_____

_____

Name: _____ Date: _____

Defining Leadership

There are many types of leaders. They can be any gender, race, age, or culture. They can have different personalities. Thinking about what makes a person a leader can help you become one, too.

Directions: An acrostic is a poem where the first letter of each line spells a word or phrase. Each line also describes the main idea. Follow the acrostic poem example to write one of your own.

> **K**eeps mean thoughts to self
>
> **I**nterested in others
>
> **N**ice to lonely people
>
> **D**iscusses things with different people

L _____

E _____

A _____

D _____

E _____

R _____

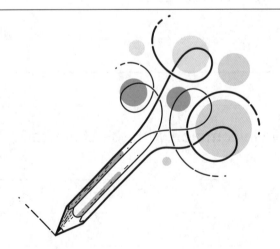

Name: _____ Date: _____

Learning from Conflict

People sometimes think conflict is bad and that it should be avoided. But that is not true. Conflict can actually be a good thing. It can help people find problems that need to be solved. A conflict might feel uncomfortable because people are disagreeing. But it can also be a tool for learning.

Directions: Read the story, and answer the questions.

Sharing a Room

Lucy and Claire's grandparents were visiting for two weeks. They were going to stay in Lucy's room, so she was moving in with Claire for a while.

The first few days were fine, but then Claire noticed Lucy's laundry on the floor and unmade bed. There were empty food wrappers and half-full glasses of water on the dresser.

"Lucy, you are such a slob!" Claire exclaimed after a week of living together.

Lucy looked hurt. "I know I'm a little messy, but there's no way I can be as tidy as you are."

"We have to figure this out," Claire said. "Can you please keep your mess on your side of the room?"

"Sure," Lucy agreed. "Can you just ignore my mess on my side until I get my room back?"

Claire nodded. "It's not a perfect solution, but that will work for now."

1. What is the conflict in the story, and how is it resolved?

_____

_____

2. What do the girls learn during their conflict?

_____

_____

_____

Name: _____ Date: _____

Focus on Neighborhood

Self-Awareness

Feelings and Actions

The way you think about yourself is powerful. Positive self-thoughts can make you feel brave. Negative self-thoughts can make you feel upset. The thoughts you have about yourself don't just affect your feelings. They can also affect how you interact with other people. Imagine a confident person and an anxious person. They act very differently. Thinking good thoughts will help you in many ways.

Directions: Explain how you would act in each situation.

1. A boy your age moves into your building. How would you act if you felt confident?

   _____

   _____

2. The kids in your neighborhood want to start a lemonade stand. How would you act if you felt like a leader?

   _____

   _____

3. A big snowstorm leaves driveways covered in snow. How would you act if you felt helpful?

   _____

   _____

4. A power outage at night leaves your home in darkness. How would you act if you felt brave?

   _____

   _____

5. A new student comes to your class in the middle of the year. How would you act if you felt friendly?

   _____

   _____

Name: _____ Date: _____

Helping Yourself and Others

Everyone needs help now and then. There will be times when you'll need to help yourself, and that is not selfish. Sometimes, when you help yourself, you can help others, too. When you need help and want to solve the problem yourself, ask yourself whether the solution can help others, too. Helping others while you help yourself is a win-win.

Directions: Write a solution to each problem that can help both you and others in your neighborhood.

1. You feel bored on a beautiful Saturday afternoon.

   _____

   _____

2. You need to make a meal, but you don't know how to cook.

   _____

   _____

3. You have permission to start a garden in an empty lot in your neighborhood, but you don't know much about gardening.

   _____

   _____

4. Write something you can do to help yourself and others.

   _____

   _____

Focus on Neighborhood

Self-Management

Name: _____ Date: _____

Focus on Neighborhood
Social Awareness

Showing Concern for Others

A neighborhood is full of people. Over time, neighbors can become friends and learn about each other's lives. They may care about each other. If one neighbor goes through something hard, neighbors can show concern. They might do it with words or actions. The acts of service don't have to be big or difficult. Sometimes, the smallest actions mean the most to the person who needs it.

Directions: Read the story, and answer the questions.

Helping Mrs. Kapoor

Everyone in Luke's neighborhood loved Mr. and Mrs. Kapoor. When Mr. Kapoor passed away, the neighbors knew Mrs. Kapoor would need help.

She did not know how to drive, so Luke's mom organized a carpool. That helped Mrs. Kapoor get to the store. Mrs. Kapoor felt lonely, so the neighbors made a schedule. Someone called her every day. Visitors came by twice a week. When her yard began to look overgrown, Luke and a few of his friends decided to help. They volunteered to cut the grass and weed the flowers.

Mrs. Kapoor was so thankful. She always made sure to have lemonade and cookies to offer to the people who helped her.

1. Why does Mrs. Kapoor need help?

_____

2. How do Luke and his friends help?

_____

3. How could you help someone in your neighborhood?

_____

_____

_____

_____

_____

Name: _____ Date: _____

Standing Up for Others

Imagine someone is being bullied or mistreated in your neighborhood. What can you do? You can offer support to the person being bullied. You might get them away from the bully or talk to them about what happened. If you feel comfortable, you can speak up for the person and tell the bully to leave. And you can always tell a trusted adult and get their help. Don't be a bystander—stand up for others.

Focus on Neighborhood

Relationship Skills

Directions: Read the story, and answer the questions.

Devon's Dilemma

Ebony could hear a dog barking as she walked through her neighborhood. As she got closer to the noise, she could see a young boy named Devon holding his dog's leash. The small dog was barking at the two older boys blocking the sidewalk.

Ebony could hear the boys teasing Devon, and saw Devon's head hanging low. She walked up to the small group.

"Hey, Devon," she said, putting her hand on his shoulder. "Do you want to let your dog meet mine? I bet they'll have fun together."

Devon nodded quickly and said, "Yes, that sounds like fun."

Ebony put her arm around him and glanced at the older boys. "See you around," she said loudly and led Devon away.

1. How does Ebony help Devon?

_____

2. Do you think Ebony did the right thing? Why or why not?

_____

_____

3. What else could Ebony have done to help him?

_____

_____

Name: _____ Date: _____

Seeking a Mediator

When two people have a conflict, they can often solve it themselves. But sometimes, they need help. Maybe the problem is too big, or they cannot agree on a solution. In these cases, the people in conflict need a mediator. This is a person who works with both people to find a solution. A mediator should be neutral. That means they are not on either person's side. A third person can be very helpful for solving all sorts of conflicts.

Directions: Create a comic strip that shows two neighbors having a conflict and using a mediator to help them solve it.

Name: _____ Date: _____

Identifying the Intensity of Emotions

When things happen, you have an emotional reaction. Imagine you hear some good news. It makes you feel happy. But not all good news is met with the same intensity. Your reaction might be a smile, or it might be jumping up and down with excitement. It's important to have appropriate reactions.

Directions: Write the emotion you would feel in response to each situation. Circle the number to describe the intensity of that feeling. Five is the highest, and one is the lowest. Then, answer the question.

1. Your friend yells at you about something that is not your fault.

      5   4   3   2   1

_____

2. You borrow a friend's book and lose it.

      5   4   3   2   1

_____

3. Your best friend invites you to go on vacation with them.

      5   4   3   2   1

_____

4. Your friend crashes their bike into a tree and gets hurt.

      5   4   3   2   1

_____

5. Can reacting too intensely be a problem? Why or why not?

_____

_____

_____

Name: _____ Date: _____

Managing Your Emotions

Friends are kind and support each other. You probably spend time with your friends and talk to them about things that are important to you. Sometimes, a friend might need your help. How could you help if a friend was upset or was feeling stressed? Imagine what you would do if you were the one feeling that way. Help your friend use the same strategies. It might be deep breathing, finding personal space, counting backwards, or asking for help from an adult.

Directions: Draw yourself helping a friend who is upset. Then, explain your drawing.

_____

_____

_____

Name: _____ Date: _____

Understanding Different Rules

Have you been to a friend's home? You probably noticed several differences between their home and yours. Their house might look different, and your friend might have a different number of siblings or pets. Their family might also have different rules. Things that are allowed at your home might not be allowed at theirs. When you visit a friend's house, it is important to know their rules. This will help you be a respectful guest.

Directions: Read the story, and answer the questions.

Jesse's House

Willow was excited to go to her new friend Jessie's house. They both loved playing basketball and video games, so she knew they would have a great time.

When she arrived, Jessie invited her back to her room. She had a TV and a gaming system in her spotless room.

"Wow!" Willow exclaimed. "Your room is so clean! Mine is always a mess. And I can't believe you have a TV. Our family doesn't have them in our bedrooms."

"Really? I guess it's not a big deal to my parents. But you have a messy room? That would never work in my house because being tidy is really important to my mom. Sometimes, I wish I could just throw things where I want."

1. What is different about Willow's and Jessie's houses?

_____

_____

2. What do they like about each other's family rules?

_____

_____

3. What rule does your family have that a friend's family does not?

_____

Name: _____ Date: _____

Focus on Friends

Relationship Skills

Developing Positive Relationships

Friends are people you can have fun with and talk to. They are there when you need help, and they are ready to comfort you when you feel sad. Developing a good friendship takes time. You have to get to know each other and discover things you have in common. You need to slowly build trust. Even after a friendship is created, it takes work to keep it going strong, but having good friends is one of the best parts of life.

Directions: Answer the questions about one of your friends.

1. My friend: _____

2. What do you enjoy about your friendship with this person?

   _____

   _____

3. Describe one thing this friend knows about you that few other people know.

   _____

   _____

4. What do you wish was different about your friendship?

   _____

   _____

5. How can you make your friendship even stronger?

   _____

   _____

   _____

   _____

Name: _____   **Date:** _____

Reflecting

Reflecting about your friendships is a good idea. To reflect, ask yourself questions and answer them. You can ask yourself who your closest friends are and why you are close to them. Think about what you do with your friends, and decide whether your friendships are healthy. Healthy friendships are kind and equal. One person does not boss around the other one. This kind of reflection can help you have strong friendships.

Directions: Draw pictures that reflect on your friendships.

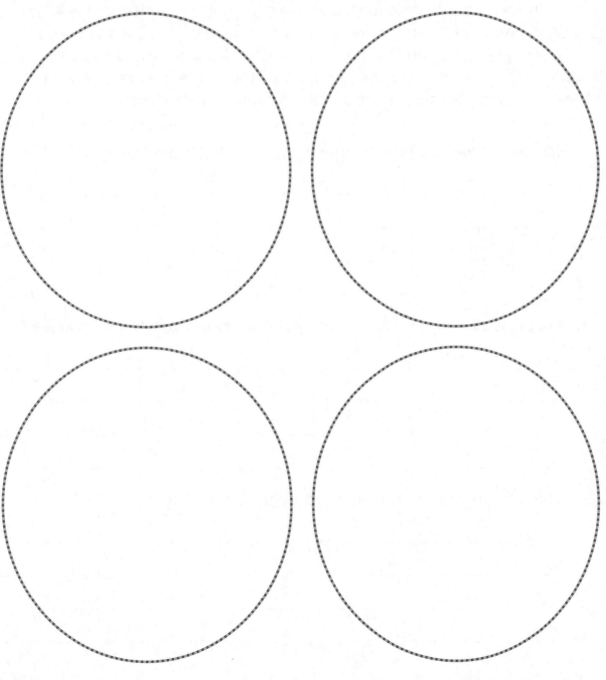

Focus on Friends
Responsible Decision-Making

Name: _____   Date: _____

Connecting Actions to Feelings

Feelings can often lead to actions. If a person feels mad, their actions might be slamming doors and yelling. But sometimes, feelings can lead to organized actions. Those actions might protest something unfair. They may even lead to new laws and bring big changes.

Directions: Read the text, and answer the questions.

Women's Suffrage

Women's suffrage (the right to vote) shows how unfairness can lead to actions. In the past, women in the United States did not have the right to vote. For years, women thought it was unfair. They protested and wrote letters. They spoke to leaders. Sometimes, they were even arrested. In 1890, Wyoming became the first state to allow women to vote.

1. How did women's feelings about voting lead to a state taking action?

_____

_____

_____

_____

2. What is something you feel strongly about? How does it make you feel?

_____

_____

_____

_____

3. What actions can you take in response to your feelings?

_____

_____

_____

_____

Name: _____ Date: _____

Setting Realistic Goals

Setting goals is important for everyone, even state governments. A goal should be realistic. It should also be specific. Imagine if your state set a goal to restore all natural habitats for animals by next month. That is not realistic. It is not specific. A better goal would be to plant 100 trees over the next year. That is both realistic and specific. When you make a goal, make sure it is something you can really do.

Directions: Read these education goals. Circle *yes* if they are realistic and *no* if they are not. If they are not, rewrite the goals to make them more realistic.

1. All students will learn a new language in one week.   yes   no

_____

2. Music students will practice 20 minutes every day.   yes   no

_____

3. Math students must get 100% on every test.   yes   no

_____

4. Physical education students will go for a run three times each week.   yes   no

_____

5. Language arts students will read a new book every night.   yes   no

_____

6. Make a realistic education goal for yourself.

_____

_____

Focus on State

Self-Management

Name: _____ Date: _____

Defining Point of View

Understanding someone else's point of view is helpful. This means you can see things from their side. It can help if you disagree about something or are confused about what someone means. Point of view is also important when looking at a map. Do you go north or south to get to the lake? It depends on where you are starting from! Your point of view is important, but it might be different from another person's.

Directions: Study the map, and answer the questions.

1. If you are in Des Moines, in what direction will you travel to get to Mason City?

   _____

2. If you are in Sioux City, in what direction will you travel to get to Fort Dodge?

   _____

3. If you are in Mason City, in what direction will you travel to get to Cedar Falls?

   _____

4. If you are in Dubuque, in what direction will you travel to get to Cedar Falls?

   _____

Name: _____ Date: _____

Providing Feedback in Communication

Recall that when two people communicate, they each have a job. One sends information. The other receives it. The receiver can give feedback. They might ask a question if they don't understand. They might nod or use a facial expression to agree. They could also make a suggestion. Giving feedback is important. It helps the sender know whether their message is getting through. It improves communication.

Directions: Read the story, and answer the questions.

The News Conference

The press room was crowded with reporters waiting to hear Governor Mensah speak. She stepped into the large room and stood at the podium.

"Thank you for coming today," she began. She saw confused looks among the faces. Some of the reporters began checking their equipment, while others cupped their hands by their ears.

Governor Mensah looked down at her microphone. "Whoops!" she said with a chuckle as she pushed a button. "My mic wasn't on. Now, we can get started."

The reporters smiled in relief. They sat back and prepared to listen.

1. What is the problem in the story?

_____

_____

2. What feedback do the reporters send Governor Mensah when she began speaking?

_____

_____

3. What feedback does she receive at the end of the story?

_____

_____

Focus on State

Relationship Skills

Name: _____ Date: _____

Focus on State

Responsible Decision-Making

Evaluating the Effects of State Laws

New laws can be like a wave. They start with one big splash that might affect a group of people in a big way. But smaller drops of water reach many other people in smaller ways. It is important to think about how a decision can impact others.

Directions: Read each situation, and answer the questions.

1. Your state wants to pass a law to change the driving age from 16 to 17.

   • Who do you think this would affect most? Why?

   _____

   _____

   • Who else would it affect? How?

   _____

   _____

   • How would it affect you?

   _____

2. Your state wants to pass a curfew law so that children younger than 12 cannot be out past 9:00 p.m.

   • Who do you think this would affect most? Why?

   _____

   _____

   • Who else would it affect? How?

   _____

   _____

   • How would it affect you?

   _____

Name: _____ **Date:** _____

Contributing to Your Country

People belong to at least one culture. The United States has countless cultures. Every one of them is special. People can share their cultures to make the country a better place. It helps people understand each other. A country made of many cultures is a lot more fun.

Directions: Draw a part of your culture. Include how it also represents your country. Then, explain your drawing.

Focus on Country

Self-Awareness

_____

_____

_____

Name: _____ Date: _____

Using I-Messages

People need to work as a team in all areas of a country. But there are many different opinions about what is right for the country. This can create conflict. When people argue, they might feel as if they are being attacked. That does not help the situation. Recall that using I-messages is a better way to communicate your feelings. Begin a sentence by sharing how you feel. It is gentler than telling the other person what they did or didn't do. When both people use I-messages, a solution is easier to find.

Directions: Rewrite each sentence using an I-message. You can change the words, but keep the general idea the same. See the example. Then, answer the question.

> **Example:** Your idea is way too complicated.
>
> I get a little confused by ideas with a lot of parts.

1. You need to keep your dog on a leash.

   _____

   _____

2. You didn't sign up to volunteer.

   _____

   _____

3. Your directions were not clear.

   _____

   _____

4. You are always late to our meetings.

   _____

   _____

Name: _____ Date: _____

Noticing Needs

People are often willing to help others. But sometimes, they don't know that help is needed. They might also think help has to be something big. But good help comes in all sizes. Small acts of kindness add up to big change. Pay attention to others, and notice what is going on. You will find opportunities to help others in small, meaningful ways.

Directions: Read the story, and answer the questions.

At the Pet Store

Shing's teacher gave his class an unusual assignment. She told the students to look for chances to help others. When Shing's mother told him they had to go to the pet store, he thought it would be a good place to look for ways to help.

In the parking lot, Shing saw a pair of sunglasses and picked them up. Inside the store, he took them to the customer service counter. Inside, he saw a woman drop a dog toy. He picked it up and handed it back to her. In the dog food section, Shing saw a man with a cane struggling to carry a heavy bag of food. Shing hurried over with a cart so the man could put the bag down.

This is fun, Shing thought to himself. He decided to pay attention and help others more often.

1. Why does Shing help others?

_____

_____

2. How do you think the people Shing helps feel? Why?

_____

_____

3. What errands do you go on? How could you help others there?

_____

_____

Name: _____ Date: _____

Communicating without Bias

Recall that bias means believing that one thing is better than another without proof. A bias assumes something to be true without really knowing. Biases often make their way into a country's language. Words can have biases. Unbiased language puts people first. It is more general. It tries to be neutral. It avoids things such as gender and race.

Directions: Study the examples of biased and unbiased language in the United States. Then, answer the questions.

Biased Language	Unbiased Language
mankind	humankind
little old lady	a woman in her 90s
cancer victim	a person who has cancer
mailman	mail carrier
congressman	member of congress
cleaning lady	

1. Why are *mailman* and *congressman* biased?

_____

_____

2. Why is *cancer victim* biased?

_____

_____

3. Why should a country strive to use unbiased language?

_____

_____

4. Add an unbiased way to say *cleaning lady* to the table.

Name: _____ Date: _____

Using Critical Thinking

There are many different types of jobs in a country, from workers in a local store to the president. People in any job need to be good problem-solvers. Problems will often arise. People have to figure out how to solve them.

Directions: Read the story. Imagine you are the president. Draw a picture showing how you would solve the problem. Then, explain your drawing.

Focus on Country

Responsible Decision-Making

Meeting with the President

The president of the United States meets with important people every day. They give the president information. They help make big decisions. Today, the president is meeting with the secretary of education. This is the person who helps make decisions about schools in the country.

The secretary wants to get rid of all standardized tests. "They are not a good way to predict future success," she tells the president. "And they are not fair for every student."

"I hear you," the president replied. "But what do we have to replace them with? How will we know if students have learned what they need to know?"

_____

_____

_____

Name: _____ Date: _____

Focus on Self

Self-Awareness

Core Values

Recall that your core values are the values that are most important to you. They might include ideas such as respect and honesty. Being responsible is also a value. These values often describe how people treat others. But it is good to treat yourself with these same values. You can respect others and also respect yourself. You can be honest with yourself. You can be responsible for doing things that are good for you. Core values are for yourself, too.

Directions: Draw pictures to show how you can treat yourself with each core value. Explain each picture.

Respect

Responsibility

_____

_____

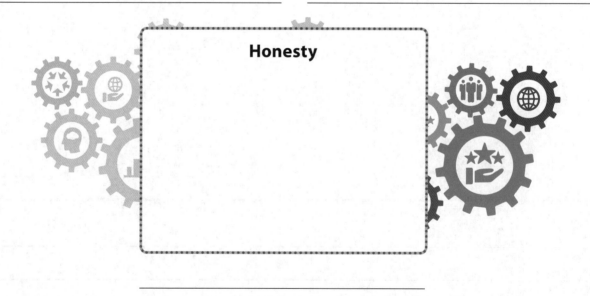

Honesty

_____

Name: _____ **Date:** _____

Setting Goals

Setting goals is a great way to accomplish tasks and skills. Some goals are small and can be met in a short amount of time, but others are large and might need to be broken down into smaller goals. Giving these smaller goals a time frame is helpful. If you want to learn how to knit, your goal might be to make a sweater. Your first small goal might be to watch a video or read a book about how to knit. Then, you might practice knitting a simple square. When you have met those smaller goals, then you are ready to work on your big goal.

Directions: Think of a big goal for yourself. It could be related to fitness, school, a hobby, or something else. Then, break down the goal into smaller ones by answering the questions.

1. What is your big goal? _____

_____

2. What is your first small goal? By what date will you meet it? You should be able to accomplish this in a few days.

_____

_____

3. What is your next small goal? By what date will you meet it? You should be able to accomplish this in a few weeks.

_____

_____

4. Next, focus on your big goal. By what date will you meet it?

_____

5. Do you think you will be able to do this? Why or why not?

_____

_____

_____

Name: _____ Date: _____

Focus on Self
Social Awareness

Showing Gratitude

Studies show that showing gratitude can make people happier. When people look for things in their lives to be thankful for, it changes the way they see things. Of course, tough things might still happen, but grateful people find the good. Some people make gratitude lists. The lists are full of big and small things they are thankful for. People, things, events, and ideas might be included in their lists. Writing things they are grateful for means they can look back at those things and remember.

Directions: Make a list of at least 10 things you are thankful for.

My Gratitude List

1. _____

2. _____

3. _____

4. _____

5. _____

6. _____

7. _____

8. _____

9. _____

10. _____

Paraphrasing

Paraphrasing is a very important tool. Imagine talking to a friend about a really good movie or book. You would not tell them every single thing that happened. You would paraphrase. Recall that paraphrasing means to share a shorter version of something. It means using your own words. It is similar to a summary. Paraphrasing a movie or book is a great way to get a friend to watch or read it, too. Just don't give away the ending!

Directions: Paraphrase a book or movie you enjoy. Be sure to share only the most important details from the story. Then, draw a picture of an important part.

Title: _____

_____
_____
_____
_____
_____
_____

Focus on Self
Relationship Skills

Name: _____ Date: _____

Focus on Self

Responsible Decision-Making

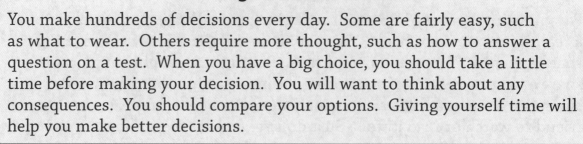

Making Better Decisions

You make hundreds of decisions every day. Some are fairly easy, such as what to wear. Others require more thought, such as how to answer a question on a test. When you have a big choice, you should take a little time before making your decision. You will want to think about any consequences. You should compare your options. Giving yourself time will help you make better decisions.

Directions: Read the story, and answer the questions.

Toy Aisle Decision

After dog-sitting for his neighbors, Henry earned $20. He was excited to see what he could buy, so his mom took him to the store the next day.

"What about this?" he asked, holding up an action figure. "Or this?" he added, pointing to a remote-control car. "Or maybe that?" he said, eyeing a chess set.

"I thought you wanted that new video game," his mom said.

"I don't have enough for that. It's $30," Henry explained.

"I don't think you're ready to make a decision. Let's go home so you can think about your choices. We can come back tomorrow if you want to buy something," his mom suggested.

"Good idea," Henry agreed. "I don't want to waste my money!"

1. What is the problem in this story?

_____

2. What do you think Henry should do with his money? Why?

_____

_____

3. When have you had a big decision to make? What did you do?

_____

_____

Name: _____ **Date:** _____

Advocating for Yourself

People like to be independent. They often want to do things for themselves. But sometimes, that just isn't possible. Everyone needs help every now and then. Asking for help when you need it is a way to advocate for yourself. You might need help with chores or schoolwork. Maybe you need help with a friendship or your emotions. Figuring out what you need and who can help you is important. Asking your family members is often a good place to start.

Directions: Answer the questions about two things your family can help you with.

1. What is one thing you need help with? _____

   _____

2. Why do you need help? _____

   _____

3. Who will you ask? Why? _____

   _____

   _____

4. What is one other thing you need help with? _____

   _____

5. Why do you need help? _____

   _____

6. Who will you ask? Why? _____

   _____

   _____

Focus on Family
Self-Awareness

Name: _____ Date: _____

Managing Stress

Yoga is a popular way to reduce stress. People can take classes at a gym or studio, or they can practice in their own homes. Yoga poses are designed to stretch different parts of the body. It is important to do deep breathing when going through poses. Yoga is something you can do by yourself, but it is fun to do it with others. You could lead a yoga session in your home. It would be a great way to de-stress with your family.

Directions: Practice the yoga poses, and answer the questions.

mountain pose   tree pose   belly breathing

bridge pose   cobra pose

1. How did you feel after doing the yoga poses?

_____

_____

2. Which pose did you like best? Why?

_____

_____

Name: _____ Date: _____

Predicting How Others Are Feeling

Words are not the only way people can communicate. Their bodies and facial expressions also send messages. You need to listen to what others say. But you need to notice nonverbal clues, too. This will help you understand what a person means even better.

Directions: Read the texts, and answer the questions.

The Phone Call

"Anyone home?" Darnell called as he walked in the door. Dad's car was in the driveway, which was unusual for the middle of the day.

Dad, Grandpa, and Darnell's brother were in the family room. His brother was sitting in front of the TV, but was staring into space. Dad was nervously pacing back and forth. Grandpa was slumped over in his chair, his head in his hands.

1. How do you think the characters are feeling? How do you know?

_____

_____

_____

"What's going on?" Darnell asked. Dad started to answer, but his cell phone rang. He quickly answered and listened to the voice on the other end for a moment. His brother and Grandpa stared at him, waiting.

Dad nodded as his face broke into a huge smile. Grandpa sat up straight in his chair and raised his arms in thanks to the sky. His brother jumped up from the couch and ran to hug Dad.

2. How do you think the characters are feeling now? How do you know?

_____

_____

_____

Focus on Family
Social Awareness

Name: _____ Date: _____

Communicating Effectively

There are many different ways to communicate. You can talk to a person face-to-face or on the phone. You can text, email, or write a letter. Each method has its pros and cons. Sometimes, one type of message makes more sense or works better in a situation. You wouldn't mail a letter to a sibling to let them know you want to ride bikes after school. Talking face-to-face would be much faster. Being able to communicate in many ways is a good skill to have.

Focus on Family

Relationship Skills

Directions: Complete the chart with three different ways to communicate. List a pro and con for each. Then, answer the questions.

Way to Communicate	Pro	Con

1. Which type of communication do you prefer? Why?

_____

_____

2. How do you think communication will change in the future?

_____

_____

Causes and Effect of Conflicts

Conflicts are natural in a family. Being able to solve them is important! One thing that can help is to think about why the conflict happened. This is the cause. Then, think about what could happen as a result of the conflict. That is the effect. Some conflicts can bring people closer together. They solve the problem and make the relationship stronger. Other conflicts are harder to solve. They might change a relationship. When possible, try to let a conflict make a good change.

Directions: Read the text. Draw how the conflict could have a positive effect on the relationship. Then, explain your drawing.

Spring Break

Sadie and Cora are excited. Spring break has just started. It's great to have time to sleep late and have fun with each other. But the girls are already arguing about whose turn it is to play video games and about the lack of privacy. The sisters love each other very much. They want this time together to strengthen their relationship, not ruin it.

_____

_____

_____

Focus on Family

Responsible Decision-Making

Name: _____ Date: _____

Linking Emotions to Behavior

Recognizing how you feel is very important. Emotions can be strong. They even have the power to change your behavior. Imagine you are already feeling angry, and a classmate bumps into you. You might overreact and yell at them. Feeling angry doesn't mean it is okay to yell. But realizing why you yelled and linking it to your anger is a great first step. It can help you be more self-aware.

Focus on School

Self-Awareness

Directions: Describe how each situation would make you feel. Then, write how that emotion might affect your behavior.

1. Your teacher has been teaching math for 20 minutes. You still do not understand it.

   How would you feel? _____

   How would you behave? _____

2. You ask your friend to play soccer at recess. She ignores you and goes to the playground with another friend.

   How would you feel? _____

   How would you behave? _____

3. You have been working on your painting in art class for two weeks. When you are finished, it looks exactly like you wanted.

   How would you feel? _____

   How would you behave? _____

4. Your teacher tells you the story you wrote is amazing. He would like to share it with the class.

   How would you feel? _____

   How would you behave? _____

Name: _____ **Date:** _____

Using a Schedule

Schedules are very helpful. Businesses use them to plan meetings, and families use them to get places on time. Teachers also use schedules. They help teachers make sure they get to all the lessons for that day. The schedule also marks when lunch or special classes will take place. Many students work better when they know when things will happen, so schedules help them, too!

Directions: Look at the daily schedule for Mr. Schneider's fourth-grade class. Then, answer the questions.

Welcome to Wednesday!

8:30 Morning Meeting

9:00 Reading

10:00 Spelling/Writing

11:00 Music

11:30 Lunch

12:00 Recess

12:30 Science

1:00 Math

2:00 Social Studies

2:40 Afternoon Meeting

3:00 Dismissal

1. How much time is spent on spelling and writing? _____

2. What happens after math? _____

3. When is music? _____

4. How long is science? _____

5. How is your daily learning schedule similar to this one? How is it different?

_____

_____

_____

Name: _____ Date: _____

Focus on School

Social Awareness

Understanding Different Rules

Sometimes, it is easy to understand why places do not have the same rules. A water park and a movie theater are very different. It makes sense that their rules are not the same. But sometimes, the same place can have different rules. Imagine an assembly in the school gym versus a basketball game. They would not have the same rules. Understanding how rules can change can help you act in an appropriate way.

Directions: Read the story, and create a set of rules for each situation.

Alone and Together

Mateo's teacher often asked students to complete work by themselves. But sometimes, they worked in groups. Mateo noticed there were different rules when he worked with others. He mentioned it to the teacher. She agreed. They thought it would be smart to write the rules for each situation.

Rules for Working by Myself

1. _____

2. _____

3. _____

Rules for Working with Others

1. _____

2. _____

3. _____

Name: _____ Date: _____

Developing Positive Relationships

People often try to create good relationships with their peers. This is how you make friends. But your relationships with teachers are also important. Teachers aren't just at school. They are also the coach of a team you play on or the person who gives piano lessons. They are all the trusted adults who are there when you need them. Having good relationships with all your teachers means you take time to learn about them. You show you appreciate them.

Directions: Answer the questions about a teacher in your life.

1. What teacher do you have a good relationship with?

_____

2. What do you like about them?

_____

_____

3. Why do you think this person became a teacher?

_____

_____

4. How can you show this person you appreciate them?

_____

_____

5. What question would you want to ask them?

_____

_____

Focus on School

Relationship Skills

Name: _____ Date: _____

Trying New Things

Trying new things can be fun and adventurous. New hobbies, new activities, and new sports are so exciting. What about books? You might have an author or genre of book you really like. But it might be great to try something new. You can ask friends what they enjoy reading. A librarian could also share new titles. Be open-minded, and you could discover a new world through books.

Directions: Draw a book you enjoy in the first box. Draw a book you are willing to try in the second box. Then, answer the question about each one.

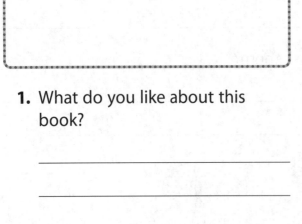

1. What do you like about this book?

_____

_____

_____

_____

2. Why do you want to read this book?

_____

_____

_____

_____

Name: _____ Date: _____

Integrity

It is important to have integrity. Recall that integrity means you are honest, fair, and try to do the right thing. Having integrity can be tough. It often takes extra effort, and you might be the only one acting that way. But the feeling you get from doing the right thing is worth it. And it is a great way to help your community and set a good example for others.

Directions: Write a paragraph about a time you did the right thing for someone in your community. Be sure your paragraph describes what happened, what you did, and how you felt. Give your paragraph a title.

_____

_____

_____

_____

_____

_____

_____

_____

_____

_____

_____

_____

_____

_____

_____

_____

_____

Focus on Community

Self-Awareness

Name: _____ Date: _____

Getting through Tough Times

No one likes tough times, but everyone has them. You have probably gone through something sad or scary. When this happens, you can get support from family and friends. One thing you can do is to practice self-talk. You can tell yourself encouraging things, think through a plan, or figure out what you should do next.

Directions: Read the story, and answer the questions.

Lost

Ethan hadn't lived in his new community long, and yesterday was the first time he walked to the park by himself. As he walked, the houses started looking unfamiliar. Ethan started to feel nervous.

It's okay. I can figure this out, he told himself. *All of the streets on the way to the park have names with a type of tree in them, so that is what I need to look for.* He turned down Hawkins Lane on the lookout for more street signs. The next street was named Sugar Creek. That wasn't right, so he kept going.

I have my phone with me, he thought. *I can call Dad if I need to.*

After another few minutes of walking, he came to Oaks Landing. *Yes!* he thought. *This is the right way. I know where I am now.* Sure enough, the park was right around the corner.

1. How does Ethan encourage himself?

_____

_____

2. Why do you think Ethan tells himself he could call his dad?

_____

_____

3. How could you use self-talk during a tough time?

_____

_____

Name: _____ Date: _____

Showing Concern for Others

One way to be a kind person is to show concern for the feelings of others. You don't have to fix their problems, but you can be encouraging or supportive. Think of people you know in your community. When they feel sad or lonely, you could say something nice to them. When they feel excited and happy, you could celebrate with them. Showing concern is a way to let people know you care.

Directions: Draw how you could show concern for each person.

---

1. Your friend's dog has been missing all day. Your friend is really scared.

---

2. The cashier at the store is acting very grumpy. You can tell he's had a bad day.

---

3. You see a classmate at the library. He is disappointed because the book he wanted is gone.

Focus on Community

Social Awareness

Name: _____ Date: _____

Focus on Community

Relationship Skills

Appreciating Cultures

Americans practice a lot of religions. They each have a special culture. Learning about cultures is a good idea. It helps you know more about the people in your community.

Directions: Read the text, and answer the questions.

Ramadan

Ramadan is a special holiday for Muslim people. It happens during the ninth month of the Islamic calendar. Since this calendar is based on the moon cycles, it is not always on the same date. But it is often in the spring.

For an entire month, Muslims fast during the day. That means they do not eat or drink. Don't worry, though. They eat a meal before the sun rises and another big meal in the evening when it is dark. Children do not fast. Neither do people who cannot for medical reasons.

During Ramadan, Muslims pray and help others. They think about the poor who do not have enough to eat. They attend services and read the Qur'an, their holy book. When the month is over, they have a celebration that lasts three days.

1. Why isn't Ramadan on the same date each year?

_____

_____

2. What do people do while they are fasting?

_____

_____

3. Think of another holiday. How is it similar to Ramadan? How is it different?

_____

_____

_____

Name: _____ Date: _____

Solving Conflicts

A community is filled with all types of people who have many ideas. There will be conflicts that must be resolved. One way to solve a conflict is with a compromise. Recall that a compromise is when people reach a solution that gives each of them part of what they want. Another type of solution is called *authoritarian*. This is when a person in control makes the decision. They are the authority. No one else has a say in what happens.

Directions: Read the text. Draw a compromise. Draw an authoritarian solution. Then, answer the question.

Fixing the Potholes

The mayor and a city council member are having a problem. Main Street has too many potholes and needs to be repaired. The mayor wants to fix them using money that was going to be used on the firehouse. The city council member wants to use money that was going to be used on the city's pool. They do not know how to solve their conflict.

Compromise	Authoritarian

1. Which way do you think is better for solving this conflict? Why?

_____

_____

Name: _____ Date: _____

Focus on State

Self-Awareness

Naming Your Emotions

Different people and places can bring up lots of ideas in your head. They can trigger memories and opinions, which can bring up feelings. Think about the state of Texas, for example. It might make you think of cowboys and horses. How do those ideas make you feel? Or think about New York. You might picture the Statue of Liberty and the business of a big city. How does that make you feel? Recognizing how certain things make you feel helps you become more self-aware.

Directions: Complete the table about various states.

State	What do you think of?	What emotion does it make you feel?
Alaska		
California		
Florida		
Hawai'i		
Kansas		
Massachusetts		
New York		
Texas		

 126960—180 Days of Social-Emotional Learning

Name: _____ **Date:** _____

Self-Discipline

State governments have budgets. They have a certain amount of money to spend, and they must plan how to use that money responsibly. Budgets aren't just for states, though. Your family might have a budget. If you earn or receive money, you should have a budget, too. Having a plan for how you spend and save your money is important. It is a form of self-discipline.

Directions: Study Jasmine's budget for the month, and answer the questions.

Jasmine's Monthly Budget

Money Earned This Month	
$10.00	mowing the lawn
$5.00	unloading the dishwasher
$8.00	babysitting neighbor's kids
$12.00	pulling weeds

Money Spent This Month	
$4.00	book
$11.00	gift for Mom
$6.00	movie ticket
$10.00	t-shirt

1. How much money did Jasmine earn this month? _____

   How much did she spend? _____

   How much does she have left over? _____

2. What do you think she should do with the leftover money? Why?

   _____

   _____

3. Why is it important to have a budget?

   _____

   _____

Focus on State

Self-Management

Name: _____ Date: _____

Helping Others

Your state has programs to help people. It provides services such as schools, police forces, and fire stations. It gives money to people who have lost their jobs or who do not make enough money to buy food. But the state cannot do everything. This is why there are nonprofit organizations. These groups raise money for things such as animal shelters, cancer research, and care for people in need. A popular way for nonprofit groups to raise money is through races. People sign up to walk or run the race. They ask for donations from their friends and families. The money goes to the nonprofits. They use the money to help others.

Directions: Imagine you are going to walk in a race to raise money for a cause that is important to you. Create a poster to advertise the race.

Name: _____ Date: _____

Influencing Others

Your state has several leaders. The governor is the main leader. There are also state senators and representatives. Leaders often have the power to influence others. They want people to work hard and do the right thing. They try to influence people to support their laws and ideas. When it is time to be elected, they hope to influence people to vote for them.

Directions: Read the speech a student who wants to be president of their class gave. Then, answer the questions.

Vote for Me!

You should vote for me to be class president. I have gone to this school for many years, and I know most of the students. I've talked to a lot of you to find out what is important to you. If I am president, I will do my best to make the changes you want.

Several students said they wanted more time at lunch. I have a plan to get students through the lunch line faster. This will give students more time to eat, even though the amount of time will stay the same.

Other students mentioned that the playground equipment is getting old. If I am elected, I will talk to the principal and try to find ways for the school to raise money to update our playground.

I hope you will vote for me to be class president. I will work hard for you.

1. What is the student trying to influence people to do?

_____

_____

2. How is the student showing they would be a good class president?

_____

_____

3. Would this speech persuade you to vote for this person? Why or why not?

_____

_____

Name: _____ Date: _____

Focus on State

Responsible Decision-Making

Evaluating Solutions to Conflict

Conflicts are common in all state governments. They also happen in businesses, families, and between friends. When a conflict happens, people often brainstorm more than one way to solve the problem. But how do they choose a solution? The people in conflict need to evaluate each one. They should consider how the solution will affect others and think about its pros and cons. When you have a conflict, look for the best solution.

Directions: Read the story, and answer the questions.

Park Problem

Mountain View State Park had a problem. Campers were leaving litter around the campground. A group of park rangers met to discuss solutions.

"I think we should put up signs," Ranger Martin suggested. "Our signs can ask campers to throw away their trash. We can even explain what happens to the wildlife when litter is left."

"I think we need to stop letting people camp here," Ranger Haga said. "When people hike or bike the trails, there are no problems. The litter is happening when people camp overnight."

1. Does Ranger Martin think of a good solution? Why or why not?

_____

_____

2. Does Ranger Haga think of a good solution? Why or why not?

_____

_____

3. Write one more possible solution. _____

_____

4. Which solution would you choose? Why? _____

_____

Name: _____ Date: _____

Celebrating Your Culture

One great thing about the United States is that it has so many cultures. There are many languages, religions, and traditions that were brought from other countries. Some people who live here now were born here. Others are immigrants. They moved here from other places. All cultures should be celebrated.

Focus on Self

Self-Awareness

Directions: Draw yourself in the space between the bubbles. Fill in the bubbles with words or phrases that share information about your culture. Then, answer the question.

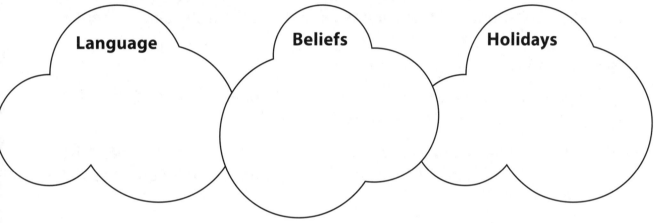

Language   **Beliefs**   **Holidays**

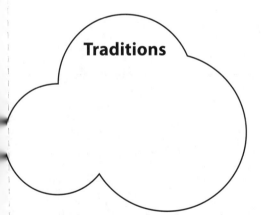

Traditions

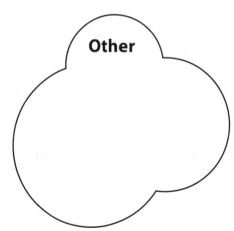

Other

1. What do you enjoy about your culture?

_____

_____

_____

Name: _____ Date: _____

Focus on Self
Self-Management

Overcoming Fear

Everyone has fears. There might be something you are afraid to try, and you may have all sorts of reasons not to do it. It takes bravery to try something new. Being brave does not mean you have completely overcome your fear. It means you try it anyway.

Directions: Read the story, and answer the questions.

The Speeding Bullet

Kele swallowed hard as he looked up at the towering roller-coaster. The Speeding Bullet opened that summer, and it was the fastest, tallest coaster in the amusement park. Kele's friends were excited to ride it, but he was really scared.

"I know the coaster is safe," he whispered to himself. "They do checks every day, and nothing dangerous will happen."

Brady could tell Kele was nervous, so he came to his friend's side. "I'll sit by you, and you can scream as loud as you want or close your eyes. I won't say anything."

The group of boys got in the surprisingly short line. In just a moment, it would be their turn to board. Kele's heart was beating fast, but he made up his mind. He was doing it.

1. How does Kele help himself overcome his fear?

_____

_____

2. How does Brady help Kele?

_____

_____

3. What types of strategies help you overcome your fears and try new things?

_____

_____

_____

Name: _____ Date: _____

Taking Others' Perspectives

You know that your emotions can affect how you act. Your emotions can affect the way other people act, too. It's almost as if feelings are contagious. Your emotion might cause you to act a certain way toward a person. Then, that person may act differently toward someone else. It is like a chain reaction. It is good to know how your behavior can affect others.

Directions: Read the story and the different reactions. Then, write how each reaction could affect Mary's sister's feelings.

Torn Shirt

Mary's younger sister borrowed her favorite shirt. It is from a vacation, so it cannot be replaced. Her sister accidentally tore a big hole in it. She comes into Mary's room holding the ruined shirt.

1. Mary jumps up off of her bed, scowling. She yells at her sister, grabs the shirt, and pushes her out of her room.

   _____

   _____

   _____

2. Mary gasps when she sees the shirt. She takes it from her sister and hugs it to herself. Tears fill her eyes when she thinks about the memories she has from the vacation.

   _____

   _____

   _____

3. Mary smiles at her sister and takes the shirt when her sister hands it to her. She pats her sister on the back and asks her to sit on the bed and tell her what happened.

   _____

   _____

   _____

Name: _____ Date: _____

Focus on Self

Relationship Skills

Active Listening

You do a lot of talking and a lot of listening every day. If you want to communicate well, you will be an active listener. Regular listening is passive. You do not do anything. You just allow the other person to talk. You may not even pay attention. Active listening is different. You have a job to do while someone else is talking. That job is to understand and remember what was said.

Directions: Answer the questions about active listening.

1. What should you do before a person begins speaking?

_____

_____

_____

2. What should you do while you are being an active listener?

_____

_____

_____

3. What should you do after the speaker is finished talking?

_____

_____

_____

4. When is it easy to be an active listener? When is it hard for you to be an active listener?

_____

_____

_____

Name: _____ Date: _____

Evaluating Consequences

Your behavior has consequences. Throwing a ball in the house could break a window. The consequence might be paying to replace it with your own money. But not all consequences are bad. Finding a missing dog would make its family very happy. It is smart to think about the choices you make and the way you behave. This can help you avoid negative consequences.

Directions: Write at least one possible consequence of each action.

Action	Possible Consequences
You are disrespectful to your parent.	
You help a teacher without being asked.	
You jump out from behind a door and scare your brother.	
You volunteer to walk dogs at the animal shelter.	
You spend all afternoon playing a video game.	

Answer Key

There are many open-ended pages and writing prompts in this book. For those activities, the answers will vary. Examples are given as needed.

Week 1 Day 2 (page 13)

You forgot to study for your science test: "I will think about what I learned during class and do my best."

Your dog is missing: "Lots of people will help us. I'm sure she's safe."

You burned the cookies you were baking: "This was my first try. Next time, I will do better."

You are performing a song for your school: "I have practiced so many times, and I know I am ready."

Your brother broke your favorite toy: "I will talk to him and find out what happened before I react."

Week 1 Day 3 (page 14)

1. sad
2. excited
3. scared
4. tired

Week 1 Day 5 (page 16)

Examples:

1. big problem; I do not know how to sew, so I would need help from an adult.
2. small problem; I can replace batteries in a toy.
3. small problem; The lid is probably in my room, and I can look for it as I clean.
4. big problem; The broken pieces are sharp and could hurt me, so I need help from an adult.

Week 2 Day 4 (page 20)

1. Aniyah's family divided up the jobs to do. The girls are working on their room, their mom is working in the kitchen, and their dad is carrying boxes.
2. Donating will help her family because their house will not have so much stuff in it. It will help others because the stuff they donate could be useful.

Week 3 Day 3 (page 24)

1. D
2. A
3. B
4. A
5. C

Week 3 Day 4 (page 25)

1. lose-lose
2. win-lose
3. win-win

Week 4 Day 1 (page 27)

close freezer door, pick up trash, hand item to child, put bread and bananas back on the shelf, give wallet to the manager

Week 4 Day 2 (page 28)

1. The committee could sell raffle tickets, have a bake sale, ask for donations, host a trivia night, or have a silent auction.
2. People could volunteer to clean the clock. People with the right skills could help repair the clock or tower.
3. It is beautiful and unique, and it's a part of the county's history.

Week 4 Day 4 (page 30)

Examples:

1. Miss Silver did research and talked to other people about the problem. Then, she presented her findings to the council and convinced them to change their minds.
2. Good leaders should be brave and honest. They should work well with other people and listen.

Week 5 Day 3 (page 34)

1. unjust
2. just
3. unjust
4. unjust
5. just

Week 6 Day 2 (page 38)

Examples:

1. I would feel like I need to jump up and down.
2. I would feel hot.
3. I would feel jittery and like I need to walk around.
4. I would feel like there is a weight on my chest and a lump in my throat.
5. You can get hurt physically, or your feelings can get hurt. If you fall off your bike, you would be hurt physically. If someone teases you, you would be hurt emotionally.

Answer Key *(cont.)*

Week 6 Day 3 (page 39)

1. She might feel happy or grateful for the help.
2. She might feel confused or upset that Dwane did not want to play with her.
3. He might be scared of the things in the show now, too.
4. He might feel annoyed or jealous of the new bike.

Week 7 Day 2 (page 43)

1. Will didn't think he could ride as well as the neighborhood kids.
2. Antony knew Will couldn't ride and asked him to practice in a friendly way.

Week 7 Day 4 (page 45)

Examples:

Sender: speak clearly, use gestures or body language, make eye contact

Receiver: look at sender, listen carefully, nod to show understanding

Week 7 Day 5 (page 46)

1. The Aldens are not getting their mail because Mr. Pruett is parked in front of the Aldens' mailbox.
2. Examples: Mr. Pruett parks his car somewhere else; Mr. Alden moves his mailbox.

Week 8 Day 2 (page 48)

1. Jamie has self-discipline because she has a plan to help her get ready for the race. She goes to bed early and gets her clothes and breakfast ready the night before.
2. He was late to practice, and she may have had to wait for him to warm up.

Week 8 Day 3 (page 49)

1. Norah and her mom took dinner to Zoe's house.
2. Example: Norah might make a basket for Zoe to take to the hospital with a book, some snacks, and coloring materials.

Week 8 Day 5 (page 51)

Examples:

1. Jack might stop playing the game with his friend.
2. Akshar might get his feelings hurt and not want to race anymore.
3. Macie might be embarrassed or angry and ask to go home.

Week 9 Day 2 (page 53)

1. Drew's mom got a job, and Drew wanted to help her cook dinner.
2. Example: He could show other people how to cook. Or he could cook a meal for someone else.

Week 9 Day 3 (page 54)

Examples:

1. shelter director: nervous about being in the middle of something; in an awkward position
2. dog owner: relieved to have his dog back
3. Ms. Pérez: surprised and sad that she will not get to take the dog home

Week 9 Day 4 (page 55)

Examples: look at the speaker, stay quiet, concentrate, ask questions, nod your head, clap when appropriate

Week 10 Day 2 (page 58)

1. fireworks begin
2. TV interview; governor's speech; students read essays; state residents share memories

Week 10 Day 5 (page 61)

Examples:

1. My family would have to install solar panels, and we might not have the money to afford them.
2. I could no longer talk with my mom on the rides to and from school.
3. I will have to find a new activity to do after dinner.
4. I will have to ask an adult every time I need to research something.

Week 11 Day 4 (page 65)

1. I can check for understanding by asking questions, asking someone to repeat themselves, looking at facial expressions or gestures, and paraphrasing.

Week 11 Day 5 (page 66)

1. Becca's idea is not a compromise because it would only make her happy.
2. Riley's idea is a compromise because both girls can get the food they want, but not at the restaurant they wanted to go to.

Answer Key *(cont.)*

Week 12 Day 2 (page 68)

1. The family's goal is to begin a vegetable garden to save money and spend time together.
2. Example: This is a realistic goal because they have given themselves enough time, and they say they have a plan.
3. Example: The family will need to learn about growing a garden. They will need to go to the store and buy supplies. They will need to dig up the area for the garden and plant the seeds.

Week 12 Day 3 (page 69)

Examples:

1. angry, frustrated
2. lonely, sad
3. stressed, busy
4. happy, generous

Week 12 Day 5 (page 71)

Examples:

Step 1: Evan lost his brother's compass.
Step 2: Isaiah could say, "I am angry you lost my compass."
Evan could say, "I am so sorry. It was an accident."
Step 3: Evan could go back and look for the compass. Evan could buy Isaiah a new compass.
Step 4: Evan will buy Isaiah a new compass.

Week 13 Day 2 (page 73)

1. Jenna could have a *school* and a *social* category.

Week 13 Day 4 (page 75)

1. Javier was being treated fairly with his learning. He had a tutor to learn English and was getting work in Spanish so he could understand what to do.
2. Tess stood up for Javier by talking to the teacher. She gave suggestions on how to help Javier make friends.

Week 14 Day 4 (page 80)

1. Gabby doesn't have a job to do in the group.
2. Example: Gabby can start mixing colors they will need to paint the sign.

Week 15 Day 3 (page 84)

1. Everyone should learn Spanish; it will help with everyday life
2. Everyone should learn science; it will help with future jobs

Week 15 Day 4 (page 85)

1. Mr. Kent wants to put more technology in classrooms for students.
2. He asked schools what they need, tried to get donations, and asked the government to use budget money for technology.
3. Example: I would vote for him because he is working hard to do what he said he would.

Week 16 Day 1 (page 87)

1. Liz did not do the right thing because she copied facts. She needs to rewrite them in her own words.
2. Taisha did the right thing because she didn't copy a drawing but used some to get ideas.
3. Jon did not do the right thing because he was not kind to the other player.

Week 16 Day 3 (page 89)

1. yes
2. no
3. no
4. yes
5. no
6. yes
7. yes
8. no

Week 16 Day 4 (page 90)

1. Leo is pressuring Jackson to get an app even though Jackson is supposed to have permission before downloading.
2. Example: I would tell Leo that I'll ask my mom about the app tonight.
3. Example: I could ask them to stop pressuring me or change the subject.

Week 17 Day 2 (page 93)

1. Mr. McPhee is using I-messages.
2. Example: Mr. Valdez seems angry and mean. His language sounds as if he's attacking Mr. McPhee.
3. Example: Mr. McPhee seems calm, but dismissive. His language sounds calm but firm in his opinion.

Answer Key *(cont.)*

Week 18 Day 2 (page 98)

Examples:

1. Yes, Kylie needs to deescalate because she is yelling and kicking things.
2. I think Jayla should turn off the video for now and suggest they try it later.
3. I would tell Kylie to take some deep breaths and to not worry about the dance for now. I'd tell her the routine is hard, and it might just take extra practice.

Week 19 Day 4 (page 105)

1. The neighbors were getting clothes, making food, repairing the home, and watching the kids.
2. Tess heard Mrs. Jackson say their photo albums were ruined, and she wants to gather photos to make a new album.
3. Example: The Jacksons will be very thankful and will think it is a wonderful gift.

Week 19 Day 5 (page 106)

1. Requiring a doctor's note is constructive because it will allow the league to continue in a safe way.
2. Stopping the league is destructive because it will not make anyone happy.

Week 20 Day 3 (page 109)

Examples:

School Rules: walk in the halls; don't touch artwork on the walls; be safe

Classroom Rules: raise your hand before speaking; finish your work; clean up your supplies

1. A classroom is where students are close together and learn, so they need rules that help students do that.
2. Different cities and states might have different situations and challenges.

Week 21 Day 4 (page 115)

1. threatening
2. sarcasm
3. judging
4. insulting

Week 21 Day 5 (page 116)

Examples:

1. I'm sorry. I kicked the ball inside after you told me not to. I will not do that anymore.
2. I'm sorry. I forgot the book after I promised I'd bring it. I will remember tomorrow.

Week 22 Day 2 (page 118)

1. violin lesson, hockey game, lunch with Grandpa
2. Tuesday the 24th at 8:00 a.m.
3. Friday the 27th at 5:00 p.m.

Week 22 Day 3 (page 119)

Examples:

1. He is confused because he is staring at instructions and parts and is rubbing his forehead.
2. She is tired or stressed out because she flopped on the couch, closed her eyes, and didn't put her stuff away.
3. She is sad because she is crying and wiping her eyes.

Week 22 Day 4 (page 120)

Examples:

1. I would point to the other person and then move my arms as if I were swimming.
2. I would tap my wrist and then act as if I were eating something off of a plate.
3. I would wrap my arms around myself as if I were cold and make my teeth chatter.
4. I would point to myself and make a heart with my hands. Then, I would act as if I were swinging a baseball bat.

Week 23 Day 1 (page 122)

1. Peter was prejudiced against Sonja because he didn't think girls could do robotics.
2. The second boy tells Peter to leave Sonja alone because they don't know anything about her.

Week 24 Day 2 (page 128)

1. Jemma is upset because the factory is closing, and both of her parents will lose their jobs.
2. She rides her bike, listens to music, writes in her journal, and talks to her parents.

Week 24 Day 3 (page 129)

Examples:

1. calm in emergencies
2. good with children
3. a leader
4. good at cooking
5. brave
6. creative
7. organized

Answer Key *(cont.)*

Week 24 Day 4 (page 130)

Examples:

1. Solution 1: Postpone trivia night until the repairs are made and the restaurant reopens.
2. Solution 2: Move trivia night to a different restaurant.

Week 25 Day 1 (page 132)

1. Marco does not have money for the shelters and does not want to tell people the truth.

Week 25 Day 3 (page 134)

1. The first person's actions show he is nervous and unsure of himself. The second person's actions show she is confident.

Week 25 Day 5 (page 136)

1. The bad behavior prevented Nora from being able to see the sculptures.
2. The situation was not fair because students with good behavior missed out on exploring the museum.

Week 26 Day 5 (page 141)

1. Claire is neat and Lucy is messy, so sharing a room caused them to fight. Lucy will keep her mess on her side of the room, and Claire will ignore Lucy's mess.
2. Example: They learn how to compromise, share open space, and accept differences.

Week 27 Day 1 (page 142)

Examples:

1. I would go introduce myself.
2. I would offer to help get things organized.
3. I would shovel the neighbors' driveways.
4. I would get some flashlights.
5. I would ask them if they wanted to play with my friends at recess.

Week 27 Day 3 (page 144)

1. She needed help because her husband passed away.
2. They cut the grass and pulled weeds.

Week 27 Day 4 (page 145)

1. Ebony made an excuse so they could both leave.
2. Example: Ebony did the right thing because she got Devon away from the bullies without getting into a fight.
3. Example: She also could have told the older boys to leave Devon alone or told her parents what happened.

Week 28 Day 3 (page 149)

1. Willow cannot have a TV in her room, but can have a messy room. Jessie's family lets her have a TV, but her room has to be clean.
2. Willow wants a TV, and Jessie wishes her room could get messy.

Week 29 Day 1 (page 152)

1. Women felt not being allowed to vote was unfair, so they took action by protesting and fighting for their right to vote.

Week 29 Day 2 (page 153)

Examples:

1. no; they will learn to count to 10 in the new language in one week.
2. yes
3. no; they will be encouraged to do their best and improve.
4. yes
5. no; they can read one chapter of a book every night.

Week 29 Day 3 (page 154)

1. north
2. east
3. south
4. west

Week 29 Day 4 (page 155)

1. The problem was that the microphone was off, and the reporters could not hear her.
2. The reporters gave her feedback that they could not hear her by checking their equipment and looking confused.
3. The reporters smiled, letting her know they could hear her.

Answer Key *(cont.)*

Week 30 Day 2 (page 158)

Examples:

1. I would feel more comfortable if your dog was on a leash.
2. I would be so happy if you could volunteer at our next event.
3. I felt confused when I tried to use your directions.
4. I feel stressed when we don't have enough time for our meetings.

Week 30 Day 3 (page 159)

1. Shing helped others because it was a homework assignment.
2. Example: They probably appreciated it because he was kind even though he did not know them.

Week 30 Day 4 (page 160)

1. They assume the gender of the person.
2. It does not put the person first.
3. Example: Language should be unbiased so it is fair to all people. Language should make all people feel included.
4. house cleaner; cleaning person

Week 31 Day 5 (page 166)

1. The problem is that Henry does not know what to buy with his money.

Week 32 Day 3 (page 169)

1. The family is worried. Pacing, slumping, hands on head, and staring off into space are examples of worried body language.
2. The family is relieved and happy because they are smiling and hugging.

Week 33 Day 2 (page 173)

1. one hour
2. social studies
3. 11:00
4. 30 minutes

Week 34 Day 2 (page 178)

1. Ethan told himself he could figure it out.
2. He was reassuring himself that he could get help if he needed it.

Week 34 Day 4 (page 180)

1. It is based on the Islamic calendar, which uses the moon cycles.
2. They pray, help others, read the Qur'an, go to services, and think about the poor.

Week 35 Day 2 (page 183)

1. $35.00; $31.00; $4.00
3. Budgets are important because they keep people from spending too much money and help them plan large purchases.

Week 35 Day 4 (page 185)

1. The student is trying to influence people to vote for them.
2. The student explains how they are listening to students' concerns, such as giving students more time to eat lunch and improving playground equipment.

Week 36 Day 2 (page 188)

1. Kele used positive self-talk to tell himself he would be safe.
2. Brady encouraged Kele and promised to sit by him.

References Cited

The Aspen Institute: National Commission on Social, Emotional, & Academic Development. 2018. "From a Nation at Risk to a Nation at Hope." https://nationathope.org/wp-content/uploads/2018_aspen_final-report_full_webversion.pdf.

Collaborative for Academic, Social, and Emotional Learning (CASEL). n.d. "What Is SEL?" Last modified December 2020. https://casel.org/what-is-sel/.

Durlak, Joseph A., Roger P. Weissberg, Allison B. Dymnicki, Rebecca D. Taylor, and Kriston B. Schellinger. 2011. "The Impact of Enhancing Students' Social and Emotional Learning: A Meta-Analysis of School-Based Universal Interventions." *Child Development* 82 (1): 405–32.

Goleman, Daniel. 2005. *Emotional Intelligence: Why It Can Matter More Than IQ.* New York: Bantam Dell.

Palmer, Parker J. 2007. *The Courage to Teach: Exploring the Inner Landscape of a Teacher's Life.* San Francisco: Jossey-Bass.

Name: _____ Date: _____

Connecting to Self Rubric

Days 1 and 2

Directions: Complete this rubric every six weeks to evaluate students' Day 1 and Day 2 activity sheets. Only one rubric is needed per student. Their work over the six weeks can be considered together. Appraise their work in each category by circling or highlighting the descriptor in each row that best describes the student's work. Then, consider the student's overall progress in connecting to self. In the box, draw ☆, ✓+ , or ✓ to indicate your overall evaluation.

Competency	Advanced	Satisfactory	Developing
Self-Awareness	Can accurately identify one's own full range of emotions.	Identifies one's own emotions accurately most of the time.	Has trouble identifying their own feelings.
	Understands that thoughts and feelings are connected.	Sees the connection of thoughts and feelings most of the time.	Does not connect thoughts to feelings.
	Can identify strengths and areas of growth.	Can identify a few strengths and weaknesses.	Can identify only one strength or weakness.
Self-Management	Can manage stress by using several different strategies.	Manages stress with only one strategy.	Does not manage stress well.
	Shows motivation in all areas of learning.	Shows motivation in a few areas of learning.	Shows little to no motivation.
	Is able to set realistic goals.	Sets some goals that are realistic and some that are not.	Has a hard time setting goals that are achievable.

Comments

_____

_____

_____

_____

Overall

Name: _____ Date: _____

Relating to Others Rubric

Days 3 and 4

Directions: Complete this rubric every six weeks to evaluate students' Day 3 and Day 4 activity sheets. Only one rubric is needed per student. Their work over the six weeks can be considered together. Appraise their work in each category by circling or highlighting the descriptor in each row that best describes the student's work. Then, consider the student's overall progress in relating to others. In the box, draw ☆, ✓+ , or ✓ to indicate your overall evaluation.

Competency	Advanced	Satisfactory	Developing
Social Awareness	Shows empathy toward others.	Shows empathy toward others most of the time.	Shows little to no empathy toward others.
	Can explain how rules are different in different places.	Knows that some places can have different rules.	Is not able to articulate how rules may change in different places.
	Can list many people who support them in their learning.	Can list some people who support them in their learning.	Can list few people who support them in their learning.
Relationship Skills	Uses a variety of strategies to solve conflicts with peers.	Has a few strategies to solve conflicts with peers.	Struggles to solve conflicts with peers.
	Uses advanced skills of listening and paraphrasing while communicating.	Is able to communicate effectively.	Has breakdowns in communication skills.
	Works effectively with a team. Shows leadership in accomplishing team goals.	Works effectively with a team most of the time.	Has trouble working with others on a team.

Comments

_____

_____

_____

_____

Overall

© Shell Education

Name: _____ Date: _____

Making Decisions Rubric

Day 5

Directions: Complete this rubric every six weeks to evaluate students' Day 5 activity sheets. Only one rubric is needed per student. Their work over the six weeks can be considered together. Appraise their work in each category by circling or highlighting the descriptor in each row that best describes the student's work. Then, consider the student's overall progress in making decisions. In the box, draw ☆, ✓+, or ✓ to indicate your overall evaluation.

Competency	Advanced	Satisfactory	Developing
Responsible Decision-Making	Makes decisions that benefit their own long-term interests.	Makes decisions that are sometimes impulsive and sometimes thought out.	Is impulsive and has a hard time making constructive choices.
	Knows how to keep self and others safe in a variety of situations.	Knows how to keep themselves safe in most situations.	Is capable of being safe, but sometimes is not.
	Is able to consider the consequences of their actions, both good and bad.	Is able to identify some consequences of their actions.	Struggles to anticipate possible consequences to their actions.

Comments   **Overall**

_____

_____

_____

Connecting to Self Analysis

Directions: Record each student's overall symbols (page 199) in the appropriate columns. At a glance, you can view: (1) which students need more help mastering these skills and (2) how students progress throughout the school year.

Student Name	Week 6	Week 12	Week 18	Week 24	Week 30	Week 36

126960—180 Days of Social-Emotional Learning

Relating to Others Analysis

Directions: Record each student's overall symbols (page 200) in the appropriate columns. At a glance, you can view: (1) which students need more help mastering these skills and (2) how students progress throughout the school year.

Student Name	Week 6	Week 12	Week 18	Week 24	Week 30	Week 36

Making Decisions Analysis

Directions: Record each student's overall symbols (page 201) in the appropriate columns. At a glance, you can view: (1) which students need more help mastering these skills and (2) how students progress throughout the school year.

Student Name	Week 6	Week 12	Week 18	Week 24	Week 30	Week 36

Digital Resources

Accessing the Digital Resources

The Digital Resources can be downloaded by following these steps:

1. Go to **www.tcmpub.com/digital**

2. Use the ISBN number to redeem the Digital Resources.

3. Respond to the question using the book.

4. Follow the prompts on the Content Cloud website to sign in or create a new account.

5. Choose the Digital Resources you would like to download. You can download all the files at once, or a specific group of files.

ISBN:
9781087649733

Notes

Notes

Notes